From My Eyes

Anchor Your Way to a *Successful*
Elder Care Business

Shelita Woods

S.H.E. PUBLISHING, LLC

FROM MY EYES

Anchor Your Way to A Successful Elder Care Business

Copyright © 2023 by Shelita Woods

For information contact:

www.shepublishingllc.com | info@shepublishingllc.com

Cover and Title Page Design by Michelle Phillips of CHELLD3 3D VISUALIZATION AND DESIGN

ISBN: 978-1-953163-67-7

First Edition: March 2023

10 9 8 7 6 5 4 3 2 1

Foreword

From My Eyes is an amazing work of one of the strongest and most intelligent women I know. After many hours of research and years of experience, this book was created by someone who not only lives this life daily as the CEO of her own senior care facility, but who also cares dearly for seniors who start as residents, but are treated as family. Her compassion and giving spirit cause her to truly give her all in this business of caring for others and I am blessed and thankful to call this phenomenal woman Mom. You can rest assured that this book is full of valuable information from one of the leading senior care facilities in Texas.

Kyendra Hobbs

Contents

Preface

My name is Shelita Y. Woods. I am the CEO of **Anchor Way Senior Care**. We are located in Crowley, Texas, near the cities of Fort Worth and Burleson. We are in a residential, serene community; no one is ever left alone in our family environment. In this book I am answering many questions that I've had over the years and I am open to answering any questions you may have after reading my story. We have been in business since

March 2008 and we custom-built a 16-bed senior care facility #103487 for our residents in July of 2014.

We provide the following: round-the-clock assistance, laundry and linen services, housekeeping, nutritious meals and great snacks, medication management, and social activities, all in a small 16-bed setting.

When the COVID-19 Pandemic approached the scene, we understood that there would be concerns regarding it as well as other infectious diseases. I am happy to say we have no positive Coronavirus issues at the facility thus far. I stand firm on keeping visitors out of the facility unless it is a visit from the family or an essential visit. I am confident that our staff "WILL" provide excellent and passionate care for the entire family. Our rates stay the same for the duration of your loved ones' stay, even if the level of care should change. This gives relief to our residents and/or their family members who are on a fixed income/budget.

We offer facility tours, and given the opportunity, you can experience a journey of love with us. In this book, we will share how **Anchor Way Senior Care** is set apart from other Assisted Living Facilities (*ALF*), both large and small.

For more information, contact us at:

Web: **www.anchorwayseniorcare.net**

Tel: **817.297.3426**

Respectfully,

Shelita Woods, *CEO, Owner & Manager*

Introduction

"All our dreams can come true;
if we have the courage to pursue them."
– Walt Disney

As an owner of a successful Assisted Living Facility (ALF) for 15+ years, I am often asked the following questions: *How can I start an elder care business of my own? How do you get funding? How did you advertise and promote your business? How did you get clients? What is a good location? How can I find staff?*

If you have these same kinds of questions, you've come to the right place. I am writing this book to pour into those who have a true passion for the elderly. I have hopes that this book will assist you in making your dream become a reality. I want to show you *from my eyes* and from my perspective, not from a 'state-to-state rules and regulations' point of view. You will need to research and educate yourself regarding the rules and regulations, but what happens when you get the keys to your facility and your first resident is secured?

This book is based on my experience on the different levels of what can occur on an actual day in the life of **Anchor Way Senior Care**. I want to focus on a specific set of circumstances. What can happen from 6:00 a.m. to 6:00 p.m.? I want to focus on what's not taught in your average annual manager's class. I call it the simple yet essential things.

There are different ways of learning. I believe learning is more effective when you see it *live in action* and on the floor. No one day is like the other and no resident is exactly the same. I am in awe of what I have experienced and have decided to use this medium to share it with the world!

I have enjoyed my journey and hope my experiences become a road map for you. Combine them with your vision, stand out, and become an exceptional home care business.

Now is your time! So please, sit back, relax, and allow me to take you down my pathway of success.

The Promise Through the Prophetic Word of God

"Promise me you'll always remember: You're braver than you believe and stronger than you seem, and smarter than you think."

—A. A. Milne

I share the promise through the prophetic word of God, because whether you are a believer or not, your path has been made. Sometimes God sends others to help lead you into the right direction. Pay attention at all times and reflect on the milestone moments in your life that has potentially set your path.

Date: March 2001
Place: Prophecy at Heavenly Gospel Church
Who: Prophetess J. M. Thompkins

• You've sat here night after night wishing you could give to the ones who did not have

• God is putting the pieces of the puzzle together

• He is going to open the windows of heaven for blessings you will not have enough room to receive

• You will be part of one of the most significant or busiest business arenas

• You will be an example of wealth for your family

Date: July or August 2012
Place: Prophecy New Breed Christian Center
(*In a Sunday night service*)
Who: Pastor D. W. Blair

• Stop looking at houses

• God knows your heart

• A 40-room facility

• It will not be as hard as it was the last time; the government will assist you

From the Above Prophecy (July or August): I immediately came home to put on paper what a 30-room facility would look like. I posted the list on my office wall, in my wallet and gave it to my Pastor. I also gave copies to several believers. By faith, I began to look for land. I found what I thought would be perfect, after traveling and being accompanied by two realtors.

Date: December 1, 2013
Place: Prophecy at New Breed Christian Center
(*Sunday morning service*)
Who: Pastor D.W. Blair

Pastor called five people out that morning and said they were about to birth some things. I was one.

• God will give you land. *I explained we had already purchased it.* He said, "Hmmm. Not that land, more land for you to build your house on."
• Not only will you build your house, but you will have a marriage retreat center
• Brother Pat (*my husband*) will have to leave the postal service
• Write the book

• You will need to go on vacation before July because it will be for rest and relaxation. That is where God will speak some things into you. You are both creative

• You will become the 2nd millionaire at this church

3

The Vision &
The Journey

Create the highest, grandest vision possible for your life,
because you become what you believe.

-- Oprah Winfrey

I had visions of owning my own business, but did not know where to begin or what I wanted to do. I prayed, thought and prayed some more; then it came to me, what I have loved to do since I was 13 years old.

When I was 13 years old, I found myself working as a candy striper at a local hospital in my hometown. I proudly walked in after school with my red and white uniform and served jello, water, drinks and snacks to elderly men and women. It gave me the greatest joy. I remember those good ole days, spending summers with my great-grandmother "Granny."

Once I became a young adult, I made the decision to attended Angelina College of Nursing, but did not complete it because I had to relocate to the Dallas/Fort Worth, Texas (*DWF*) area. Thinking back, my only clinical rotation was telemetry, which deals with heart attack, stroke patients, and primarily the elderly.

As I searched for nursing classes in the DWF area, I found there was a waiting list and I knew that waiting could possibly result in the prior nursing classes that I'd taken to expire. If that happened, I would lose my current credits. I did not want to start over, so instead, I landed a job at a bank.

I built a career at the bank and I held employment there for a total of 29.5 years. However, in year 27.5, I found my niche. While at work, a friend walked into my branch and I found out I was her son's manager. During our hugging and reuniting, she told me she no longer had her florist business, but that she was a realtor. I told her of my desired business startup and that was the best thing I could have ever done.

We would begin using our lunch breaks to look for an Assisted Living Facility (ALF) aka care home for the elderly. I desired a new care home on a corner lot, and the name of that care home would begin with the letter "A." A couple of months would pass, and the official opening day of March 28, 2008, became a reality!

Three years later, in 2011, a second nursing home (*next door to the first one*) became available. This was a blessing, especially since the first one was full with residents. I met with another realtor since the original one had retired. I needed to find another care home with more beds which could accommodate more residents. I had no luck.

In 2013, I received a piece of mail that read, "*We buy houses.*" I hardly looked at junk mail, but this time I did. I pulled up the website looking for homes with at least ten bedrooms. I figured, well, if they have homes, they must have land. I called because the website had land that was 2.5-acres. The person that answered the phone shared that there was a larger lot around the corner from that one. My son and I jumped in the car and went to find the lot at 5+ acres. It was almost dark, and I could see the trees on the street welcoming me to my new care home. The breeze caused the tree limbs to bid me hello.

The realtor I contacted to secure this property was rude. He wanted to charge me a 6% fee, but he didn't know that I had a background in banking. I begged to differ and argued that there was no dwelling on the land, so he could only charge a 3% fee. He threatened that I had better have the money on that very day, which was

November 22, 2013, or I would lose the lot. He further told me that I could not put a business on the lot. That led me to request the deed, and as I began to read it, I found what I was searching for. The property was not zoned. I almost wanted to laugh out loud at him. Instead, I praised God for His favor. On another note, the lender was another gift of favor that God sent my way. I was approved on the spot and we moved forward. I paid cash for the land, which made instant collateral. *GOD IS AWESOME*!

On January 2, 2014, the builders broke ground. THE DREAM THAT GOD REVEALED TO ME OF THIS VERY BUILDING BEING BUILT was happening before my eyes. I would watch as they completed Phase I, II and III. For hours, I would watch the concrete trucks, the builders, the framework and the bricks take shape. I would watch the workers during my lunch break, but I couldn't eat my lunch because I was so overwhelmed and excited at the same time. In the framework, right up front, I saw three crosses. I knew then that God had all things under control.

The building was completed in May of 2014. The state came out to inspect, after which we had to make a few changes and adjustments. Finally, we moved into our newly designed-by-God commercial facility in June 2014.

As if that is making you go 'whaaaaaat?', I recall looking out the window or the front door of my house. I could see another care home across the way. After a while, I kept wondering, 'What is God trying to show me?' So on one fine Monday, after doing some shopping, I decided to visit the facility. I rang the doorbell and the owner answered reluctantly. We talked briefly, during which, I decided to ask if she would be willing to move and sell me her care home. The home was not on the market. To make a long story short, I now own the home where I can look out my window and see all that is happening at the facility. *GOD is AWESOME*!

In 2016, my mother fell ill and soon required more care than usual. She moved in with me, but she wanted to be independent. After visiting some Senior Apartments and Assisted Living Facilities in the area, it did not take long to see that pricing was ridiculously high and would possibly increase annually. Pleasing my mother, I thought, '*We have the land and the space. Why not just build one?*

I reached out to a lender. His words were, "*let's do it!*" So here we were again. The builder's broke ground on January 2, 2018!!! The first tenants were a couple from California. They wanted to move items in, but the builders had not finished the clean-up and walk-through. In May of 2018, Phase IV was complete; Mom moved into apartment #107 and the couple moved into apartment #101. To this very day, the quadplex is full of tenants. I made it easy for them without rent hikes and the worry of utility bills. We even pick up their trash. One payment takes care of everything. I love our elderly.

I got divorced in 2019, which has opened new ideas for me regarding the safety and security of our elderly generation. As a current Assisted Living Facility owner for 15+ years, there are many things I wish to share with individuals who have a passion for this industry. This book is dedicated to all the loved ones who have gone on before me. Eva Moye, my amazing great-grandmother, was the first elderly person I loved and lost. Her legacy inspired me to begin the business initially.

I remember my dad telling me to make a dollar and save a dime. He reinforced that I should never take on more than I can handle. He always told me how proud of me he was. My mother showed me how to be a lady, cook, clean and care for my family.

I had so much love growing up. Above all, God has shown me favor. I am grateful for that. This is why I am on this journey of sharing my knowledge with you. It is long overdue.

I ask God to breathe His breath of life upon these pages and allow it to sustain until, Amen.

Introduction to Anchor Way Senior Care

Aging at home is not always an option for senior adults, especially when their safety can be compromised. The idea of change is not always well received, especially if moving to a new environment is the solution. Making this decision is not easy. The thought of transitioning from normal to the unknown can be frightening for you, your family and your loved one. Recognition of timing is almost always easy to detect. The feelings of fear and anxiety that come with the territory are not welcomed. Honestly, placing your trust in an organization that you are not familiar with, and receiving care from people that you don't know, could spike your anxiety instead of calm it. **Anchor Way Senior Care** was designed and built with these feelings in mind.

Our Mission

Our mission is to be an anchor for the elderly; give stability and security on which we place dependence for safety and comfort all within a small family environment.

Caring is what we do best! We are a family-owned establishment founded simply on the basic belief that it is our responsibility to love and care for the fathers and mothers who enter our doors. Our business is based on the principle that our hearts are *anchored* with a call to always honor our residents, your loved ones, with dignity and respect. We are committed to partnering with you to provide the quality care that you expect and that your loved one deserves.

4

Passion,
Setting the Foundation,
The Operation &
A Personal Touch

"Why fit in when you were born to stand out."

-- Dr. Suess

March 28, 2008, I received the keys to my first Anchor Way Care Home Facility. Immediately, fear set in. I remember it like it was yesterday. I left the title company thinking, *"Now what? What have I done?"* I walked inside to proudly but nervously look around an empty home with no furniture, dishes, food, supplies, or residents. I still held a career with Chase Banking Center with 21 staff and wondered how I would do both and succeed. It took me a while to realize what I had done. Being the competitive person I am, after a few hours, I hit the road getting the things I would need, much like moving into my own home. I gave God a great big **THANK YOU!!!**

To begin the preparations for the operation of my care home, I first stopped by my house to pick up a few necessities, stopped by garage sales, and picked up a few pieces of furniture and groceries from several stores. Things were coming together. Arriving back at the property, I cleaned and disinfected the facility before bringing things in. Soon after, I started to unpack items from my vehicle. Many items I'd purchased along this journey, such as towels, rugs, lamps, etc.

It was only a matter of time before I created my website; it was simple, but mine. My next mission involved searching for vendors for lawn services, electricity, telephone, internet and city water, after which I began looking for residents. I would gladly give my business cards to almost everyone I would see. I made flyers and shared them with friends, neighbors and people out and about. Eventually I included faxing the flyers to other facilities.

To be on the safe side, it was imperative to study the state of Texas' rules and regulations. Requirements included taking a computer-based training, following the floor plan, and hanging state board documents that are visual in the entryway. I worked on the application process for licensing while, at the time, meeting goals for my local Chase Banking Center.

It was not until October of 2008 that I got my first resident. I was the -- employee at my facility all while still working at the bank! The day before Ms. A was to move in, I ran into an old bank employee. I hired her on the spot to work while I was at the bank. When my shift was over at the bank, I would go to the facility, then get up and do it all over again. This took place for two years. It was trial and error; prep and cook three meals and three snacks per day, managing medications, activities, etc.

PASSION

I asked in my heart and mind; *how can I help the world? What is my purpose?* I believe we are born, live, get old, and pass away somewhere along that path. I knew I did not have the desire to care for babies; I would not be in a hospital environment, and I would not work at a morgue or funeral home. At 13 years of age, it brought me joy to sit at the feet of elderly people.

So, I now ask you, what gives you life and what is your passion? If it is not caring for the elderly, their families, their children, your staff, the state, your reputation, integrity, etc., walk away now. Find your purpose and find your passion.

Why would you want to open a Senior Care Facility?
First and foremost, you will not be able to simply sit

back and enjoy this ride. Opening a business takes time, commitment and passion. Your success depends on you! This may involve you taking on the sales, operations, service, and a financial position, all in one. You always want to *inspect what you expect*. I want you to be familiar with what is going on in your community and with your facility at all times.

What experiences have you had that would warrant your desire to become a business owner? Keep in mind; increasing your experience in this area will take a lot of your time. If you are not ready for that, walk away now. There will be times when you have just arrived home, you're relaxed with a hot plate of your favorite foods. You kick off your shoes, recline your chair, then, the phone rings. It is your staff calling regarding an emergency. You must leave your meal, get dressed, collect the facts, call the professionals, the family and rush to the facility as soon as you can. Another call could consist of someone not reporting to work. You have called your pro re nata (*PRN*) staff, as well as your full-time staff, and no one can report to work for coverage. You must leave immediately to cover the shift.

How organized are you? If your current space is in chaos and disorganized and you cannot meet deadlines, walk away now. You will need certain files for the state to view when they come for an inspection. Your files/binders MUST be in order. We will speak about which binders you will need and what should be inside them.

Do you normally meet deadlines ahead of time? You will wear MANY HATS, especially in the beginning stages. There are things you must do by certain dates, such as payroll, menus, activities, doctor visits, forms, medication sheets and so on. These, more than likely, cannot wait until tomorrow. *How will you handle it*?

What might be considered the most challenging areas of focus & what are some ways of addressing the challenges?

Your greatest challenge first and foremost will be staffing. In the 15+ years that I've been in this business, I've found absolutely no remedy for this. People come and go. Pay is one of the issues; you must charge a resident enough to compensate your staff. However, depending on your location, that my cause you to have empty beds if you charge a family too much. Residents may not be able to afford your pricing. It is a balance I had trouble mastering because sometimes, no matter what you do, some employees will not be satisfied.

There are days you question yourself, *is it me?* You will have staff with different personalities and mindsets. You will always deal with attitudes, days needed off; attendance issues, people not getting along, too much time sitting down chatting and not spending quality time with the residents, or simply not following directions. I had staff who would not even complete a full shift. Prepare yourselves. I had so many potential employees who had some good interviews, but I am not sure who showed up for work. The workdays and shifts agreed upon would change, some of the staff worn wrinkled uniforms; they sit down at the dining room table for seven of the eight-hour shift, etc. I am not sure why people don't want to commit to the employment as agreed.

During family tours, potential resident's family would inquire about turnover. Answer honestly. My decision to terminate a staff member is usually due to attendance issues, lack of obtaining a TB test (*a test that screens for tuberculosis and for tuberculosis diagnosis*), required vaccines, and rarely, but so, not following instructions. You want to groom someone to see *from your eyes*, but often, that does not happen due to having a paycheck being the reason they applied. They must have a strong passion for the kind of work we do.

It is shocking when a staff will try to reason with a resident or respectfully disagree when obviously it is simpler to follow along and not agitate a resident when it is known they have dementia; reporting things they say or do. It is important to educate your staff in order to help them better serve your residents.

Are you self-motivated? You must be in order to be successful. There will be days that you might ask yourself, *what in the world have I done????* You have the state, the staff, the resident and resident families to contend with on a professional timely manner daily. Moreover, do you take care of things quickly OR put things off until tomorrow? That won't cut it and you may be entering the wrong business.

If you are a Registered Nurse (*RN*) who is interested in having your own facility, that would be great! The state does not mandate that you to have an RN on staff. You may utilize home health and hospice if the family is willing, and the resident qualifies. The physician will give you an order for evaluation and admission. The company will come and if the resident is an appropriate fit, the family will sign consents. You are there to make sure the home health and hospice is doing what they promised the family they would do.

What types of preparation would you advise for anyone wanting to follow in your footsteps? Be focused and positive that an assisted living business or any business is what you want. Work hard then you may play hard.

Is it truly your passion or is it about the money? Be sure it is truly your calling because if it is, everything should go smoothly. There will be life issues, but you will be able to overcome them. If this is your endeavor, do not let anyone or anything stop you. Things will happen and perhaps discourage or distract you. Keep pressing forward. There are families who need you.

SETTING THE FOUNDATION

We often strongly desire to become entrepreneurs, yet we do not know where to begin funding. My father always told me to make a dollar and save a dime. He told me never to take on more than I could handle alone. I heard him early on in life. Remember, a lender desires to lend to those who will pay it back under the terms and conditions mentioned and agreed upon in the loan. Visualizing your business, writing your plan, evaluating the cost and creating a simple budget is an excellent practice. You must save to get started. You must have some form of funding on your own and good, strong credit. Most banks will not lend to new businesses. They will ask for three years of personal and business tax returns. They will know if you are worthy of becoming a customer. Not only that, but they can also verify your history or track record by your business name registration. I first established ONE credit card in the business name. Thereafter, I took a home equity loan on my house to pay off all my debt. I worked at Chase for two years to help fund my business while caring for **Anchor Way Senior Care** home.

If you have good credit, it may be easier to get started. Therefore, I later established a line of credit. This is my favorite tool because it is revolving, as long as you use the funds and pay them back. I spoke with someone I knew from my hometown who had her own assisted living facility to get pointers, additional information, forms and do's and don'ts. There are grant writers available, but I did not use one. Most grant donations are geared toward nonprofit businesses. I am a for-profit business.

In addition, if you don't have good credit, I am unaware of other resources. I would stress the importance of putting cash aside until you can step into your true passions. Start small. You do not have to have a 16-bed facility immediately. I had one small home with six residents first in 2008. In 2011, I obtained a second home that had 5 residents. As the years passed, my prices increased. Then I built the current location and expanded it to 16 beds in 2014.

Where would you place your facility? Location is everything. I believe I touched on this before. You want to do your research on where you will be. Things to keep in mind are parking, size, other facilities near you, the look of the properties around you, land size, curb appeal, new or old, square footage, etc., as well as avoiding Home Owner Associations (HOAs).

What location is good enough? Purchasing land would be my first choice. I have had both a newly built home, an existing home, then finally I purchased land to develop and avoid the things I did not like at the smaller houses, such as small bathrooms, doors that are not wide enough for wheelchairs or carpeted floors where residents could trip and fall. Moreover, if you have land and it is paid in full, you may use that as collateral for your newly designed build of your facility.

What hospital locations are needed? It would be best if you familiarized yourself with the hospitals in the area. During your family interview/tour, they may also tell you their wishes. This should be part of your questions during an interview and time with the potential family.

Business name/type? I would suggest a Limited Liability Company (*LLC*) or S-Corp. You may easily set this up on your own or utilize a Certified Public Accountant (*CPA*). If you select sole proprietorship and are sued, a lawsuit may entangle all your assets, not just the business. I suggest you keep it all separate. Remember, this is a serious business dealing with the lives of the elder community. Obtain general and professional liability insurance as well as insurance for your dwelling. Payroll companies offer workers' compensation. It would be a good thing to have.

Who will be in ownership? I am 100% owner and always have been. Sometimes friendships, courtships and partnerships begin great then we become separated for whatever reason. You do not need to start a company together and then risk things going sideways after two years in. It will not be easy and can lead to a wild rollercoaster ride. If you follow my lead, you can limit many hiccups.

Should you have a CPA? You should have a CPA to track your income and debt while providing a safe and secure way to file your taxes. A CPA can also assist you in filing your Employer Identification Number (*EIN*), LLC and S-Corp.

Proper titles in a business are as follows: Chief Financial Officer (CFO), Chief Executive Officer, (CEO), Administrator, Owner, or Manager. You may be any combination of these. The state of Texas says you must have a manager, assistant manager, dietician and caregivers. A caregiver or manager, or assistant manager may serve as the dietician.

A Chain of Command in an
Assisted Living Facility may look like this:

Owner..........

       Manager.........

              Assistant Manager.............

                   Caregivers.............

How does collateral work? Collateral depends on the price of your upcoming facility. *Note:* never start building until the state receives a copy of your plans and approves them. Then move forward. If not, you may find that you will not pass inspection or must make significant changes before you are issued a provisional license. Find a commercial or residential lender, depending on zoning.

Have you checked to see if there are other facilities near you? You would want to know who is local. Are they large or small? What would make a family choose you? It would help if you also had facilities near you for a haven; for evacuation purposes.

How large is your property? You should seriously consider five acres and approximately ten thousand square feet.

How large do you plan to be? The maximum for this class is 16 beds, small type B. Currently, in Texas, 17 beds and more significant are considered oversized.

Will you own or lease? I would suggest owning because a landlord could decide to sell at any time, raise your lease fee or not make the state-required repairs to the property. MAKE SURE YOUR PROPERTY PASSES AN INSPECTION before you sign a lease or buy. You do not want to establish your address and then have to relocate or close due to the above reasons.

Have you checked with your community liaison to see if your city will allow a small assisted living facility in the city of your choice? Before you purchase an assisted living facility, you have to find out from the planning and zoning commission of your city if it is permissible. In some instances, you may have to obtain an occupancy approval letter. I would suggest you seek property that is not zoned because you have the option of securing a residential or commercial property for your assisted living facility.

Will you serve all men or all women or both? If both, how will you separate them? This will depend on how much care you tend to provide. Type A residents can evacuate in an emergency within 13 minutes without assistance. Type B cannot and will need help with activities of daily living.

What type of residents will you serve? Will you have residents who need total care or assistance? There are Type A and Type B residents. Understand the differences before your interview. An interview process with the family of a new resident may include the resident. Most of the time, the family members will be the responsible party.

How will you fund your business? If you have never owned this type of business before, you may want to utilize savings, personal line of credit, personal credit card or inheritance. Never spend more than you NEED (*more debt than income*), and never use more than 40% of your credit limit. This may lower your credit score.

How is your credit? If you cannot manage your own personal credit now or an existing business currently, again, you may want to walk away or work on mastering this first. To become reputable, you will need to utilize a commercial lender. Financial companies or investors need two to three years' tax returns, profit and loss reports, business plans and personal banking records.

They will need to see that you are worthy of their funding and that they may count on you to pay it according to the agreements set forth.

What overhead costs and fees does a facility expect monthly/annually? The essential overhead cost is much like your own home but more money; mortgage, utilities, office supplies, groceries, equipment, décor, cleaning supplies, bedding, appliances, insurance, and vendors, to name a few. There is a fee for your licensing.

How do you secure workers? As mentioned, finding loyal employees can be challenging and very stressful. You have some people who work for a paycheck only, and not for the passion of elder care. Some may be both. There is no easy solution to this. Remember to *inspect what you expect*. Have frequent trainings and open communication, such as a group text.

How many workers are needed? The number of workers will depend on the number of residents you have and the care plan for each resident. At 16 residents, you may want to utilize at least three. You must complete a form to provide for each resident's family tour at the time of the contract.

How would you pay yourself and your employees? I utilized Automatic Data Processing (*ADP*) for payroll and retirement needs. They take care of all tax records, W2s, reports, etc. Utilize a time clock as well.

Costs per month (budget)? After completing your plan to set up your business, you will set a budget. You will estimate what funds you receive and, the debt you have acquired, the business net worth. Additional costs would include repairs, installations that the state requires, training, and supplies that may include small and large equipment purchases.

Many have inquired how often does the state come in to check proper procedures? The stat will come in to check whenever there is a complaint and/or when there is time for a required inspection to renew your license.

Should I use referral companies to begin getting residents? Referrals are great to have. However, some companies will charge you a hefty fee. Word-of-mouth referrals are always the best. Initially, when no one knew who **Anchor Way Senior Care** was, I had to search, hand out flyers, and give out business cards. I had to attend marketing meetings and grand openings of large facilities. After year two, it was mainly word of mouth mainly.

Some referral agencies will consider you once they know who you are, but there is a fee for all move-ins. There is no fee for the family. If you take care of your residents and establish a reputable website and business cards, then a logo people will refer to you or find you sooner or later. Do not depend solely on any one thing. It takes all of them to keep your beds filled.

Is insurance mandatory? Insurance is not mandatory in Texas; however, I suggest you get commercial insurance to cover your investment and professional liability.

What are some of the safety issues? Several come to mind: electrical cords must be out of the way to avoid falls. Windows must be kept unblocked to escape if needed. When residents move, your staff should assist them, especially in a type B facility. This will help limit falls. You may utilize bed alarms, fall mats, and other tools to help keep residents safe. Turn in residents who cannot turn and reposition themselves every 1-2 hours. If a resident is incontinent, toilet them every 1-2 hours.

THE OPERATION

The three most vital pillar points essential for success in operations are as follows: (1) You must be motivated and set your policy and procedures to where EVERYONE FOLLOWS DAILY; do not allow any staff to change or deviate from your vision; (2) You must know the rules and regulations of the state and follow them. Stay up to date with changes. Once you fall behind, it isn't easy catching up, which may cause you to become overwhelmed and burned out; (3) You must show your passion from the heart. **<u>No one should be able to tell your story the way you do.</u>**

What are the most significant pressures & liabilities that exist within daily operations? There are many pressures and liabilities. You will need an emergency planning book which is available for a fee. You'd have to plan for preventing falls, staffing/scheduling, death, wanderers, medication management, finances, transportation, care, fires, storms, sleep deprivation, and stress, to name a few.

Who oversees medicines? An assistant manager, manager, or a designated caregiver. You may even decide to hire a certified medication aide or have a tech to manage medications. If normal staff is given the responsibility, you must audit the medications at the time you set in your *policy and procedures manual.* Your medication records should include all the following information: resident's name, medication, dosage, route, pharmacy, physician, drug number, and the number of pills. This must be an ongoing training to avoid medication errors.

How many meals per day? A good number is three hot meals and three snacks. This will be determined once you get residents and what time they like to wake up in the mornings, such as breakfast at 8:00 am, lunch at noon, and dinner at 5:00 pm. Allow your residents approximately one-and-one-half hours to eat and socialize. There may be times when you have to assist or feed a resident. You may have to adjust their diets to soft foods, no sugar added, diabetic diets, pureed diets, etc. Your menu will be created in advance and usually designed by the manager. Unfortunately, it would be expensive to have several choices, but it is also good to have an alternative for those who do not like what is being served. It a good idea to answer those questions during your interview/tour with the family. Ask what the resident's likes and dislikes as it pertains to food.

Grocery shopping & keeping enough food on hand is a priority. Establish a credit card to use for all purchases.

This will make it easy for your CPA to gather your transactions for bookkeeping. A menu must be prepared in advance. Normally two weeks. I suggest monthly breakfast, lunch, and dinner meals and meal times. In your interview with the potential resident's family, it is food time to ask about the diet and likes/dislikes as it pertains to foods. Incorporate that into your future menu. Small facilities more than likely do not have a chef or nutritionist; therefore, all staff must be able to cook tasteful meals.

Are outside professionals needed? There may be mobile physicians, Home Health Agencies, Hospice Agencies, as well as podiatrists and Dentists who will market you in your area. This is another reason you want your facility/community to be appealing and your residents to be well cared for.

Is there a criterion for a type of resident or the number of residents you can have per room? The answer to this question will depend on the state you are licensed. There are criteria for type A and type B facilities. Please keep this in mind when you are purchasing your location. Again, be cautious about renting and purchase because a landlord may hike your rent because you are doing well, sell your property, or change your lease agreement causing you to uproot your resident and their family members' lives.

Seriously consider whether you will take in residents with colostomy bags, catheters, nasogastric tubes, G-tubes, etc. These are serious caregiving diagnoses and are not to be taken lightly.

In case of an emergency, should a protocol be put in place? Yes! You will prepare an emergency evacuation binder for illness, storm, or death. It's best to place it where all staff knows where it is and what to do. Call the manager if there is an illness, fall, fire, power outage, storm, death, or stranger danger. Storms are scary. Plan and know where your safe place will be. Know which staff is responsible for what task. In case of death, the manager should call Hospice, if applicable, call the police, if appropriate, contact the responsible family member/party for the resident, and one of them will reach the coroner's office. Try to have all funeral plans in place for each resident as well. There will be times you must call 9-1-1 to send your residents out. Your emergency book should include the following: policy on Covid-19, evacuation plans/posters, your temporary location, and your transport plans. Your haven location must be able to accommodate your residents. The emergency book must also include signed documentation, a contract with the transport companies, medication sheet for each resident (*two copies*), and contact numbers for all resident's families, physicians, home health care, Hospice, utility companies, and emergency phone numbers.

The manager is responsible for contacting the facility you are transporting residents. The manager and assistant manager will gather the medications, clothes, and emergency evacuation containers which contain food for at least 7 days' worth of meals, eating utensils, water, etc.

Should the owners be available 24/7? Yes, it would be best for you to know what is happening at your facility.

In addition, although no certifications are needed, to assist the elderly, training of all of the staff is needed and some of the training include: as manager, you must take an annual online class and an annual manager's course with a reputable, approved company. The manager in collaboration with the state will determine how many employees should work with the residents per shift. I would suggest two per shift if you are a small 16-bed facility. If you acquire a large facility with 17+ residents, I recommend having more staff available. One of the biggest complaints I hear is there is not enough staff at the facilities. This will vary from state to state.

What are the protocols to take in the case of a resident dying on one's shift? This is not an easy task. You will need to know if a resident is full code (*use cardiopulmonary resuscitation – CRP*) or Do Not

Resuscitate (*DNR*). If full code, you will call the family, call 911, and 911 will contact the coroner to come and pronounce the deceased resident. If this is a home health or Hospice situation (*DNR*), you will call 911 after contacting the family. Usually, a resident who has a DNR they have been on Hospice. If a nurse is on staff and at their bedside, the nurse will call you, Hospice, and the family. It is up to you whether to go to the facility. However, a good manager would be there to support the family.

This seems to be an overwhelming responsibility. Is it best to have committees in place to maintain successful daily operations? I do not believe you "need" a committee if you have a great team of support in your staff. However, it would not hurt to have a committee. This is not an easy business. Your residents' lives are in your hands; they depend on you. You are their voice, eyes, ears, legs, etc. Please remember that.

When hiring, how important is the social network background (FB/IG posts, etc.) of applicants? It is not mandatory, but you may find it interesting. You can find out a lot about a person by scrolling through their social media. Remember they will be a representative of your brand. Every staff member must have an annual criminal history/background check and a nurse aide registry check.

One thing to focus on in orientation is to clarify your expectations. You would be surprised what people do not do or know; how to answer the phone correctly, how to answer the door, or how to escort or see someone out of the building. Your staff will need to know how to monitor the residents at all times; look for breathing, choking, or changes. Staff should try to keep residents from falling or reaching across the dinner table for someone else's food. Staff must be able to be attentive; pull the shirt/blouse down to avoid exposing a resident. Hand a resident a glass of water if you hear them coughing from a dry throat. If they are asking you a question, stop, focus, and inquire. They should see if and how they can assist the resident. Stay alert. Spend time speaking with the resident. Polish nails, brush hair, and massage the shoulders to make them feel welcomed and loved. When the shift begins, go to each resident and do a wellness check and see if all is well. The type of facility you want to have, is one that always shows love to your residents.

Staffing, depending on size, may look like this: mornings, evenings, nights, and weekends staff shifts. You may design your staff shifts as you wish, depending on what you want. For example: 6am-2pm, 2pm-10pm and 10pm to 6am. You may try 7am-3pm, 3pm-11pm, or 11pm-7am. You may also do 7am-7pm and 7pm-7am.

The staff will have 1.5 hours of training each quarter. Staff is trained 4.0-hour orientation before servicing a resident. Then they must observe caregiving for 16.0 hours before working with a resident alone.

Keep all staff informed of everything that could change daily at a facility on a day-to-day basis. We have a group text only to discuss residents. We train while on the floor; if a manager or assistant manager sees something that must be corrected, coaching happens immediately. It is sometimes difficult to keep employee morale up when you do not work as a team. When there is discord, the residents are aware of and feel it. This is the time that we support them in living their best lives. If you are positive upbeat, and treat employees with respect, be on time with each pay period, and always communicate professionally with your staff. Make the same choices for each employee. If you do not, it may come back to haunt you. Peace in the home is important. If not, you are like many other facilities. You want to be different. Wow, every tour that comes your way.

The employee turnover rate is often stressful in this industry. Because the employee turnover rate is high, it is important to find staff in the caregiver business and those who genuinely care and have a passion for helping the elderly. You will have those with other motives, much like any other business or company.

What methods can be used to encourage morale? Recognition, gifts, bonuses, cards, and verbal praise will go a long way. Think of things that make you feel good about reporting to work daily. You will be documenting after their 90 days of employment, which will be a great time to show awards and staff meetings annually.

In addition, you may want to utilize a management company to staff your facility. There will be a fee for this service. Many agencies will contact you but be mindful of your budget. The employees they offer you will only get a portion of that fee. The rest will go to the employment/placement agency.

Take extra measures for the facility to ensure client safety. You should have quarterly trainings for your staff. You should also utilize videos, home health nurses, hospice nurses, and other professionals in your arca to teach staff. Often common sense is not common. There should be no chords in the resident's path, no rugs, avoid thick carpets, avoid clutter and excess furnishings. Keep an eye on your residents. An accident can happen within seconds. An open floor plan is ideal for this type of business. You want to see what is going on and where your residents are. Do frequent checks on them to see if they need your assistance.

As proprietors, are you available when Hospice scenarios initially arise? You should be. This is your vision. Your staff would need to be very strong to function the way you do; *"From My Eyes."* They may not make the same decisions as you, and there could be an issue that may have been avoided. You can train your staff and include the reasoning behind taking a certain action over the other, in the midst of a situation, the right decision is not always made. Again, be that support.

How many hours are necessary for proper oversight? As an owner, in the beginning, you will put in 50-60 hours because you are learning and getting set up.

If you plan to be an owner-manager, you are never off work. The state requests the manager works 40 hours per week on sight and is readily available in case of an emergency and for random visits by the state.

Most facilities have been known to have some very bad odors. Keep that to a minimum. When a resident has a bowel movement, discard it immediately. Keep a large, more significant trash receptacle at the rear door or somewhere with easy access out the back door **IMMEDIATELY**! Please do not allow your residents to soil their clothes. Take all residents to the restroom every 2 hours to check their underwear and/or to allow them to relieve their bowels or bladder. This will help residents avoid constipation and urinary tract infections.

How does transportation to appointments or evacuations work? Some facilities offer transportation to appointments. I suggest you carefully consider this due to liabilities while transporting them. You will need this for new residents coming to your facility and for evacuation purposes. Have at least three different transport services and three to four safe havens for emergency evacuations.

Medication management is one of the most important things you will do for your elderly community. A medication sheet is set up for each resident. You must record all the information from the initial bottles of medicine on the sheet. For new medications, after admission or medication changes, you must have a written physician's order before managing the medication. Know the difference between managing and supervising a medication vs. administering it.

You must keep your paperwork private and in order. You must file all folders with sensitive information behind a locked door and in a secure area. If you are not available when the state arrives, an assistant manager or designee should be able to access these records.

Are families allowed visitation? Of course. However, it is up to you to create set times or not. It would be a good idea to have a beginning and cut-off time due to staff having busy peak times such as meals, getting up, or going to bedtimes. Establishing a policy would help, especially since many infectious diseases exist today.

A PERSONAL TOUCH

A family interested in your services will call and ask questions via telephone or email. YOU have 5 minutes to wow them. Try and get the family member into your facility so that they may get a feel for your vision. Give them a date and time block you have available. I would suggest not discussing numbers over the phone. Schedule the tour. Be prepared. Be early for your appointment. Confidence is everything, DO NOT stumble over your answers. Make notes (*announce that you will be taking a few notes*). Be engaged. Know the name of the family and the potential resident. Call them by name. Follow up within 72 hours but do not become pushy or aggressive. Do not promise a family or resident anything you cannot make happen.

What is the time frame for your business opening day-to-day? The time frame for your business opening day will vary per person. It depends on YOU! Levels of care will vary: some residents may need skilled care. Some residents may be incontinent of the bladder/bowel. Please keep in mind, you will have to provide care for people's loved ones, and your staff will have to clean and change them. Things that are a considerable responsibility are anyone who is bedfast and a physician has stated they may not get out of bed, insulin-dependent residents, tube-fed residents, Nasogastric (*NG*) tubes, gastric tubes, colostomy, catheter, respirators, and people who may be violent to themselves or others. I would avoid these situations unless you and your staff are well trained.

Where does the family of the residents fit into the operations? A family member is simply that. They are not just a family member to the resident but should become like family to you and your staff. They are key. They will assist you with the assessment plan for their loved one, they will visit, and they may bring special snacks that are not on the menu but that the resident likes. If they prefer a specific pharmacy that does not deliver, they will have to pick the medications up. They may provide clothes, shoes, and medications. Other things may be added or subtracted depending on your contract with the family. The family will follow any facility rules, such as communicable disease protocol. Please make these things clear during your interview and tour. Your pricing should be based on what you offer, your budget, location, building, and level of care.

What is allowable at the facility? Allowing residents to speak with their families via iPad or a smartphone may be a great idea. You could implement this as a Friday activity. I love seeing their faces light up, both the family and the resident. There are civic groups, high schools, and community or 4 yr. colleges, with many of these groups who want to come. Vo-Tech schools with horticulture programs or culinary programs. Often students will come for free.

Is it common practice to counsel patients/family members who depend upon Medicaid/Social Security on rules/income parameters that may affect the patient's ability to continue receiving benefits (I.e., if the cash value of the client's insurance or belongings exceeds $2,000, they can lose benefits). In a private care home, this usually does not apply. You are more than likely going to be private pay. You may utilize savings, long-term care insurance, or assistance from children or spouse.

Is it a good idea to solicit local services? You may want to solicit the services of a local mobile podiatrist, physician, dentist, etc. Medicare and or private insurance may pay for most of these services. Be clear that they are not part of your business and have the families complete the necessary documentation for the companies, releasing your facility of any liabilities.

What outside activities can we offer? Picnics, sitting on the patio or deck, planting in a raised garden or pots, bird watching, family visits, games, pet therapy, or simply taking in the breeze with a glass of cold iced tea or lemonade are great outside activities to offer.

I, for one, do not believe in the elegance of a building that a resident can no longer enjoy. The facility should be according to the needs of the resident you serve. Bed alarms, floor mats, great lighting, books, warm cozy blankets, good food, and quality care far outweigh chandeliers, a spa, and swimming pools.

On-site security or random police patrol is optional. This is not a bad idea, but in small communities, to avoid higher costs, it is not likely. When searching for your location, keep this at the top of the list.

Beauticians/stylists/haircuts are optional. Depending on the type of service your resident desires, you may charge additional service fees or write a check and pay the stylist.

What does work-life balance look like? When you are passionate about your work, this task that some deem simple becomes challenging, especially in today's society. So, I am creating this read for you. Try your best to have a good work-life balance. The ability to hire the right person/people, get them trained, and retain them is a great option. Take a chance on others. Otherwise, the work-life balance will be out the door.

What general services can you provide?

The general services that can be provided by the facility/community are as follows:

- Activities of daily living
- Linens
- Laundry; please wash laundry for each resident separately. Do not lose laundry.
- Meals/snacks
- Medication management
- Activities of daily living
- Showers
- Light housekeeping
- Observations and incident reporting

What happens during move-in? AT MOVE IN, make the new resident and family members feel welcome when they enter the doors for the first night and every night in the first three days at your facility. Meet them in the entryway with cake, balloons, the on-shift staff or the manager and assistant manager, if possible. Make it a grand event! They are making huge changes, and you must make them feel that being in your community was the best move ever!

The Manual

5

ANCHOR WAY
SENIOR CARE, LLC BINDER

Job duties of staff:
1. **RESIDENT**
   - Disclosure Receipt
   - Photo
   - DNR OR FULL CODE
   - Admission record
   - Advance Directives
   - Sex offender registry (done annually)
   - POA, Guardianship (If applicable) or any other legal documents
   - Individual Resident Assessment (annually and as changes develop)
   - Disclosure statement (give to a visitor as well when they tour)

- Resident Service Plan (annually and as changes develop)
- Records from any/all hospital/Dr. visits within 14/30 days
- Copy of insurance, SS card, and ID
- Resident/ Provider Bill of Rights
- Policy on Restraints and Seclusion
- Funeral home information if available and family is able to discuss.
- Emergency information packet

2. CONTRACTS
- The contract you negotiated with the family, signed.

3. EMPLOYEE (tab for each employee)
- Employee application
- Personnel Policy and Procedure Packet
- Background check; nurse aide registry and criminal checks; (done annually)
- W2
- I-9
- Personnel Packet
- Proof of TB test
- Photo ID and Photocopy Social Security #

- 90 day and annual review as well as any other coaching/merit reviews

4. **EMPLOYEE TRAINING** (see pages 33-36 in TALA training book; Section C)
- QUARTERLY TABS: sign in sheet/date for all attendees, what you will discuss, post test

5. **PAYROLL**
- Monthly tabs; file copies of all paycheck stubs

6. **TIME SHEET OR TIME CLOCK**
- Copy of each employee time recorded & signed/dated for the entire year, keep for 10 years

7. **OBSERVATION/INCIDENT REPORTS**
- One binder available for employees to complete, date, detail and sign and give to the manager for filing (kept in manager's office)
- Another binder with blank forms for them to use (available for employees)

8. SIGN IN SHEET

- Create a sign in log PLACE AT THE ENTRANCE for everyone who enters and exits (not including employees)

- **Texas Workforce**
- Any documents received from them for workers comp files…. etc.

- **MEDICATION SHEETS** (MAR)
- Resident tabs with medications listed and time to take meds. It should include the medication name, date, pharmacy, physicians name, # of pills sent, route, and
  - instructions on time and how to take the medication.

- **LIFE SAFETY BOOK**
- ***Tabs should be the following:
- DADS Inspections
- Sprinkler system
- Sprinkler system contract
- Sprinkler system semi-annual inspections
- Fire alarm certificate
- Fire alarm contract

- Fire alarm inspection by City or County (annual)
- Fire drill recap
- Fire drill report
- Annual pest control
- Monthly fire extinguisher check
- Monthly battery check
- Monthly and annual exit sign check
- Emergency lighting test

- Policies: emergency procedures for hurricanes, tornados and weather related storms, safe handling for oxygen, smoking policy, resident/provider bill of rights, restraints and seclusion, advance directives, delegation of authority for the management of personal funds (if applicable), general operational policies, missing resident policy, infection control, fire safety, emergency procedure for extreme heat, emergency housing agreement, emergency management plan, emergency transportation agreement, electronic monitoring sign (also in each bedroom), electronic monitoring sign at front and back doors, drug testing policy, Assisted living

Disclosure Statement (never promise what
you will not provide on this form),

JOB DESCRIPTION - ATTENDANTS

Qualifications:

- Sufficient formal education to enable the
performance of daily tasks with the
understanding of what is involved. Personality
attuned to the
requirements of meeting need of the infirm and
aged.   Previous   experience   helpful,   but   not
essential. Full-time facility attendants must be
at least 18 years old or a high school graduate.

Duties and Responsibilities:

- Always ensure the safety and well-being of all
residents. In emergency situations, call
ambulance or fire department as needed.
- Assist residents as required and as directed by
the manager in bathing, grooming, dressing,
etc. Always promote the maximum amount of
independence
from all residents always. Encourage them to do
as much as possible for themselves.

- Cook and serve meals. Follow menu as posted. Always ensure that cold foods are served cold and hot foods are served hot.
- Clean residents' rooms and do laundry per schedule.
- Keep all living areas, bathrooms, kitchen and dining areas clean at all times.
- Supervise resident's medication. Ensure that residents receive their proper medication at the proper time.
- Receive messages and relay these to the manager in a timely manner.
- Keep manager updated on any changes in the status of the residents' emotional physical, or psychological state.
- Refer questions or complaints on the Home to the manager.
  Be instructed in six hours of continuing education annually.
- Other job duties as assigned by the Manager.

I WILL GET A TB TEST within 10 days of employment.

Signature_____

Date _____

I _____will **not** allow family members to read the text due to HIPPA.

I HAVE READ AND UNDERSTAND THE NEW
COVID-19 GUIDELINES, POLICY AND
PROCEDURE,
THE RED BOOK "EMERGENCY
PREPAREDNESS PLAN". I WILL follow all
rules and regulation as printed in this policy and
procedure.

SIGNATURE: _____

**PROVIDE A COPY OF DRIVERS LICENSE
& SOCIAL SECURITY CARD.**

**TB TEST DUE PRIOR TO 10 DAYS OF HIRE
PLEASE INTIAL PAGES THAT DO NOT REQUIRE
SIGNATURE AND PLEASE SIGN AND DATE PAGES
THAT REQUIRE A SIGNATURE
SEE JOB DUTY LIST AND FOLLOW
MARCH 28,2008**

**I PLEDGE TO ALWAYS EXEMPLIFY
PROFESSIONAL BEHAVIOR WHILE EMPLOYED
@ANCHOR WAY SENIOR CARE; I will be
trustworthy. I will care for the residents with passion
and patience.
I will be WATCHFUL, APPROACHABLE,
FRIENDLY, HELPFUL, POSITIVE, CHEERFUL,
AND ATTENTIVE to all residents and resident families
always. I PLEDGE TO REMAIN FREE OF VALID
RESIDENT AND RESIDENT FAMILY
COMPLAINTS. IF AT ANYTIME these characteristics
are not met, I understand the possibility
of immediate disciplinary actions and or termination.**

*Signature*_____

Table of Contents

EMPLOYEE ORIENTATION

(date)

1. _____Orientation for four hours in the ANCHOR WAY SENIOR CARE, LLC

resident fact sheet, #1-12. The expectations of the facility, the needs of each resident, and reviewing the Personnel packet.

(date)

2. _____ Sixteen hours of on-the-job supervision and training in aiding with the activities of daily living, resident's health conditions and how they may affect provision of tasks, safety to prevent accidents and injuries, emergency first aid procedures, such as the sudden change in physical and/or mental status, managing dysfunctional

behavior: behavior management, including prevention of aggressive behavior and de-escalation techniques, or fall prevention, or alternatives to restraints. in reporting of abuse and

neglect, confidentiality of resident information, universal precautions, conditions about which to notify manager, resident's rights, and emergency evacuation.

(date)

3. _____ Emergency Preparedness Plan and Drill

4. _____FIRE DRILLS, FIRE BOX, FIRE EXTINGUISHERS, EVACUATION, STORM, THE RED BOOK

5. _____ Safety Rules

6. _____ Abuse and Neglect Policy (Senate Bill 9)

7. _____ Criminal Investigation Check

8. _____ I-9

9. _____ W-4

10. _____ Personnel Policies; ATTENDANCE & PERFORMANCE

11. _____ 4-hour orientation In-service on Minimum Standards

12. _____ Job Description; 401K

_____

Employee Signature   **Date**

Facility Representative: _____

Signature: _____

Date _____

1.INTRODUCTION

1.1 Handbook Disclaimer

The contents of this handbook serve only as guidelines and supersede any prior handbook. Neither this handbook, nor any other policy or practice, creates an employment contract, or an implied or express promise of continued employment with the Company. Employment with ANCHOR WAY SENIOR CARE LLC is "AT-WILL." This means employees or ANCHOR WAY SENIOR CARE LLC may terminate the employment relationship at any time, for any reason, with or without cause or advance notice. As an at-will employee, it is not guaranteed, in any manner, that you will be employed with ANCHOR WAY SENIOR CARE LLC for any set period of time.

The Company has the right, with or without notice, in an individual case or generally, to change any of the policies in this handbook, or any of its guidelines, policies, practices, working conditions or benefits at any time. No one is authorized to provide any employee with an employment contract or special arrangement concerning terms or conditions of employment unless the contract or arrangement is in writing and signed by the president and the employee.

1.2 Welcome Message

Dear Valued Employee,

Welcome to ANCHOR WAY SENIOR CARE LLC! We are pleased with your decision to join our team.

ANCHOR WAY SENIOR CARE LLC is committed to providing superior quality and unparalleled customer service in all aspects of our business. We believe each employee contributes to the success and growth of our Company.

This employee handbook contains general information on our policies, practices, and benefits. Please read it carefully. If you have questions regarding the handbook, please discuss them with your supervisor or the MANAGER.

Welcome aboard. We look forward to working with you!

Sincerely,

The MANAGER

NOTE: *Special Note: please park in employee parking. never park in the front circle. the other alternative is on the street.*

STAFF TRAINING

(4) Staff training. The facility must document that staff members are competent to provide personal care before assuming responsibilities and have received the following training.

(A) All staff members must complete four hours of orientation before assuming any job responsibilities. Training must cover, at a minimum, the following topics:

(i) reporting of abuse and neglect.

(ii) confidentiality of resident information.

(iii) universal precautions.

(iv) conditions about which they should notify the facility manager.

(v) residents' rights; and

(vi) emergency and evacuation procedures.

(B) Attendants must complete 16 hours of on-the-job supervision and training within the first 16 hours of employment following orientation. Training must include:

(i) in Type A and B facilities, aiding with the activities of daily living.

(ii) resident's health conditions and how they may affect provision of tasks.

(iii) safety measures to prevent accidents and injuries.

(iv) emergency first aid procedures, such as the Heimlich maneuver and actions to take when a resident fall, suffers a laceration, or experiences a sudden change in physical and/or mental status.

(v) managing disruptive behavior.

(vi) behavior management, for example, prevention of aggressive behavior and de-escalation techniques, practices to decrease the frequency of the use of restraint, and alternatives to restraints; and

(vii) fall prevention.

ALZHEIMER/DEMENTIA TRAINING

(a) A facility must adopt, implement, and enforce a written policy that:

(1) requires a facility employee who provides direct care to a resident with Alzheimer's disease or a related disorder to successfully complete training in the provision of care to residents with Alzheimer's disease and related disorders; and

(2) ensures the care and services provided by a facility employee to a resident with Alzheimer's disease or a related disorder meet the specific identified needs of the resident relating to the diagnosis of Alzheimer's disease or a related disorder.

(b) The training required for facility employees under subsection (a)(1) of this section must include information about:

(1) symptoms of dementia.

(2) stages of Alzheimer's disease.

(3) person-centered behavioral interventions; and

(4) communication with a resident with Alzheimer's disease or a related disorder.

ANCHOR WAY SENIOR CARE, LLC
10805 W CLEBURNE RD
CROWLEY, TEXAS 76036

Health & Safety Manual - Fire Safety

4.3 <u>Race and Pass</u>

IF YOU DISCOVER A FIRE – REMEMBER:

R - RESCUE /REMOVE anyone in immediate danger
A - Activate the Manual Fire ALARM
C - CONFINE the fire (close the door)
E - EXTINGUISH small controllable fires/or EVACUATE

P - PULL the pin
A - AIM the nozzle at the base of the fire
S - SQUEEZE handle
S – SWEEP from side to side

1.3 Changes in Policy

Change at ANCHOR WAY SENIOR CARE LLC is inevitable. Therefore, we expressly reserve the right to interpret, modify, suspend, cancel, or dispute, with or without notice, all or any part of our policies, procedures, and benefits at any time with or without prior notice. Changes will be effective on the dates determined by ANCHOR WAY SENIOR CARE LLC, and after those dates, all superseded policies will be null and void.

No individual supervisor or manager has the authority to alter the foregoing. Any employee who is unclear on any policy or procedure should consult a supervisor or the MANAGER.

2. General Employment

2.1 At-Will Employment

Employment with ANCHOR WAY SENIOR CARE LLC is "at-will." This means employees are free to resign at any time, with or without cause, and ANCHOR WAY SENIOR CARE LLC may terminate the employment relationship at any time, with or without cause or advance notice. As an at-will employee, it is not guaranteed, in any manner, that you will be employed with ANCHOR WAY SENIOR CARE LLC for any set period of time.

The policies set forth in this employee handbook

are the policies that are in effect at the time of publication. They may be amended, modified, or terminated at any time by ANCHOR WAY SENIOR CARE LLC, except for the policy on at-will employment, which may be modified only by a signed, written agreement between the President and the employee at issue. Nothing in this handbook may be construed as creating a promise of future benefits or a binding contract between ANCHOR WAY SENIOR CARE LLC and any of its employees.

2.2 Immigration Law Compliance

ANCHOR WAY SENIOR CARE LLC is committed to employing only United States citizens and aliens who are authorized to work in the United States.

In compliance with the Immigration Reform and Control Act of 1986, as amended, each new employee, as a condition of employment, must complete the Employment Eligibility Verification Form I-9 and present documentation establishing identity and employment eligibility. Former employees who are rehired must also complete the form if they have not completed an I-9 with ANCHOR WAY SENIOR CARE LLC within the past three years, or if their previous I-9 is no longer retained or valid.

ANCHOR WAY SENIOR CARE LLC may participate in the federal government's electronic employment verification system, known as "E-Verify." Pursuant to E-Verify, ANCHOR WAY SENIOR CARE LLC provides the Social Security Administration, and if necessary, the Department of Homeland Security with information from each new employee's Form I-9 to confirm work authorization.

2.3 Equal Employment Opportunity

ANCHOR WAY SENIOR CARE LLC is an Equal Opportunity Employer. Employment opportunities at ANCHOR WAY SENIOR CARE LLC are based upon one's qualifications and capabilities to perform the essential functions of a particular job. All employment opportunities are provided without regard to race, religion, sex, pregnancy, childbirth or related medical conditions, national origin, age, veteran status, disability, genetic information, or any other characteristic protected by law.

This Equal Employment Opportunity policy

governs all aspects of employment, including, but not limited to, recruitment, hiring, selection, job assignment, promotions, transfers, compensation, discipline, termination, layoff, access to benefits and training, and all other conditions and privileges of employment.

The Company will provide reasonable accommodations as necessary and where required by law so long as the accommodation does not pose an undue hardship on the business. This policy is not intended to afford employees with any greater protections than those which exist under federal, state or local law.

ANCHOR WAY SENIOR CARE LLC strongly urges the reporting of all instances of discrimination and harassment, and prohibits retaliation against any individual who reports discrimination, harassment, or participates in an investigation of such report. Appropriate disciplinary action, up to and including immediate termination, will be taken against any employee who violates this policy.

2.4 Employee Grievances

It is the policy of ANCHOR WAY SENIOR CARE LLC to maintain a harmonious workplace environment. ANCHOR WAY SENIOR CARE LLC encourages its employees to express concerns about work-related issues, including workplace communication, interpersonal conflict, and other working conditions.

Employees are encouraged to raise concerns with their supervisors. If not resolved at this level, an employee may submit, in writing, a signed grievance to the MANAGER.

After receiving a written grievance, ANCHOR WAY SENIOR CARE LLC may hold a meeting with the employee, the immediate supervisor, and any other individuals who may assist in the investigation or resolution of the issue. All discussions related to the grievance will be limited to those involved with, and who can assist with, resolving the issue.

Complaints involving alleged discriminatory practices shall be processed in accordance with ANCHOR WAY SENIOR CARE LLC's Sexual and other Unlawful Harassment Policy.

ANCHOR WAY SENIOR CARE LLC assures that all employees filing a grievance or complaint can do so without fear of retaliation or reprisal.

2.5 Internal Communication

Effective and ongoing communication within ANCHOR WAY SENIOR CARE LLC is essential. As such, the Company maintains systems through which important information can be shared among employees and management.

Bulletin boards are posted in designated areas of the workplace to display important information and announcements. In addition, ANCHOR WAY SENIOR CARE LLC uses the Intranet and email to facilitate communication and share access to documents. For information on appropriate email and Internet usage, employees may refer to the Computer, Email, and Internet Usage policy.

All employees are responsible for checking internal communications on a frequent and regular basis. Employees should consult their supervisor with any questions or concerns on information disseminated.

2.6 Outside Employment

Employees may hold outside jobs if the employee meets the performance standards of their position with ANCHOR WAY SENIOR CARE LLC.

Unless an alternative work schedule has been approved by ANCHOR WAY SENIOR CARE LLC, employees will be subject to the Company's scheduling demands, regardless of any existing outside work assignments; this includes availability for overtime when necessary.

ANCHOR WAY SENIOR CARE LLC's property, office space, equipment, materials, trade secrets, and any other confidential information may not be used for any purposes relating to outside employment.

2.7 Anti-Retaliation and Whistleblower Policy

This policy is designed to protect employees and address ANCHOR WAY SENIOR CARE LLC's commitment to integrity and ethical behavior. In accordance with anti-retaliation and whistleblower protection regulations, ANCHOR WAY SENIOR CARE LLC will not tolerate any retaliation against an employee who:

- Makes a good faith complaint, or threatens to make a good faith complaint, regarding the suspected Company or employee violations of the law, including discriminatory or other unfair employment practices;

- Makes a good faith complaint, or threatens to make a good faith complaint, regarding accounting, internal accounting controls, or auditing matters that may lead to incorrect, or misrepresentations in, financial accounting;

- Makes a good faith report, or threatens to make a good faith report, of a violation that endangers the health or safety of an employee, patient, client or customer, environment or general public.

- Objects to, or refuses to participate in, any activity, policy or practice, which the employee reasonably believes is a violation of the law.

- Provides information to assist in an investigation regarding violations of the law; **or**

- Files, testifies, participates or assists in a proceeding, action or hearing in relation to alleged violations of the law.

Retaliation is defined as any adverse employment action against an employee, including, but not limited to, refusal to hire, failure to promote, demotion, suspension, and harassment, denial of training opportunities, termination, or discrimination in any manner in the terms and conditions of employment.

Anyone found to have engaged in retaliation or in violation of law, policy or practice will be subject to discipline, up to and including termination of employment. Employees who knowingly make a false report of a violation will be subject to disciplinary action, up to and including termination.

Employees who wish to report a violation should contact their supervisor or SHELITA WOODS directly. Employees should also review their state and local requirements for any additional reporting guidelines.

ANCHOR WAY SENIOR CARE LLC will promptly and thoroughly investigate and, if necessary, address any reported violation.

Employees who have any questions or concerns regarding this policy and related reporting requirements should contact their supervisor, the MANAGER or any state or local agency responsible for investigating alleged violations.

3. EMPLOYMENT STATUS & RECORDKEEPING

3.1 Employment Classifications

For purposes of salary administration and eligibility for overtime payments and employee benefits, ANCHOR WAY SENIOR CARE LLC classifies employees as either exempt or non-exempt. Non-exempt employees are entitled to overtime pay in accordance with federal and state overtime provisions. Exempt employees are exempt from federal and state overtime laws and, but for a few narrow exceptions, are generally paid a fixed amount of pay for each workweek in which work is performed.

If you change positions during your employment with ANCHOR WAY SENIOR CARE LLC or if your job responsibilities change, you will be informed by the MANAGER of any change in your exempt status.

In addition to your designation of either exempt or non-exempt, you also belong to one of the following employment categories:

Full-Time:

Full-time employees are regularly scheduled to

work greater or equal to 40 hours per week. Generally, regular full-time employees are eligible for ANCHOR WAY SENIOR CARE LLC's benefits, subject to the terms, conditions, and limitations of each benefit program.

Part-Time:

Part-time employees are regularly scheduled to work less than 40 hours per week. Regular part-time employees may be eligible for some ANCHOR WAY SENIOR CARE LLC benefit programs, subject to the terms, conditions, and limitations of each benefit program.

3.2 Personnel Data Changes

It is the responsibility of each employee to promptly notify their supervisor or the MANAGER of any changes in personnel data. Such changes may affect your eligibility for benefits, the amount you pay for benefit premiums, and your receipt of important company information.

If any of the following have changed or will change in the coming future, contact your supervisor or the MANAGER as soon as possible:

- **Legal name**

- **Mailing address**
- **Telephone number(s)**
- **Change of beneficiary**
- **Exemptions on your tax forms**
- **Emergency contact(s)**
- **Training certificates**
- **Professional licenses**
- **<u>WE COACH BY TEXTING SO PLEASE LET US KNOW IMMEDIATELY IF SOMEONE ELSE HAS YOUR CELL PHONE OR YOU HAVE CHANGED NUMBERS!</u>**

<u>Employee Infection Control</u>

All personnel suspected of having an infectious skin lesion or disease shall be required to see their personal physician before being allowed to return to work. Employees are encouraged to report all illness and institute treatment without delay.

If you make an error, simply draw one line through the error and re-write the correct Information.

Failure to do so <u>*will*</u> cause a delay in your

pay. (1st-15th and 16th through the end of the month) **IF YOU HAVE QUESTIONS DO NOT HESITATE.**

PROPERTY DESTRUCTION

I, _____, understand that if I destroy intentionally or accidently damage any portion or equipment, walls, property of

ANCHOR WAY SENIOR CARE Assisted Living Facility I will be held responsible for the total replacement or repair of said property.

($150 per incident for employees)

*SIGNATURE*_____

*DATE*_____

SMOKING POLICY OF ANCHOR WAY SENIOR CARE

OUR FACILITIES ARE *NON-SMOKING*.

<u>No smoking</u>

is allowed inside/outside the buildings including

the garage, front and back yards. This policy applies to all Residents, Staff and Residents Family Members. Failure to abide by this policy may result in loss of privileges of entering the facilities. Staff may smoke in their vehicles or in the back field of the property near shed, if it is available.

Thank You,

ANCHOR WAY SENIOR CARE, LLC
Management

Please sign and acknowledge.

Signature_____

Date _____

JOB DESCRIPTION - ATTENDANTS

Qualifications:

Sufficient formal education to enable the performance of daily tasks with the understanding of what is involved. Personality attuned to the requirements of meeting needs of the infirm and aged. Previous experience helpful, but not essential. Full-time facility attendants must be at least 18 years old or a high school graduate.

Duties and Responsibilities:

Always ensure the safety and well-being of all residents. In emergency situations, call ambulance or fire department as needed.

Assist residents as required and as directed by the manager in bathing, grooming, dressing, etc. Always promote the maximum amount of independence from all residents. Encourage them to do as much as possible for themselves.

Cook and serve meals. Follow menu as posted. Always ensure that cold foods are served cold and hot foods are served hot.

Clean residents' rooms and do laundry per schedule.

Keep all living areas, bathrooms, kitchen and dining areas clean at all times.

Supervise resident's medication. Ensure that residents receive their proper medication at the proper time.

Receive messages and relay these to the manager in a timely manner.

Keep manager updated on any changes in the status of the residents' emotional physical, or psychological state.

Refer questions or complaints on the Home to the Assistant Managers.

Be instructed in six hours of continuing education annually.

Other job duties as assigned by the Manager.

FOLLOW ALL HOUSE RULES, POLICY AND PROCEDURES AT ALL TIMES.

Attendance:

Being late, tardy, or absent effects everyone. Be on time. If you need time off, YOU are responsible for clocking in and out.

******CALL IN PROCESS******

There are 2 types of call ins.

2 hours before your scheduled shift (SICK)

1 MONTH in advance written request for time off (VACATION, WEDDING, DAYS OFF…. ETC)

I. WHEN YOU WILL BE LATE FOR YOUR SHIFT

YOU MUST CALL: *THE ASSISTANT MANAGER* and verbally SPEAK

DO NOT TEXT to the supervisor and verbal tell the <u>Assistant Manager</u> that you will be late for your shift and what time you expect to arrive.

2. WHEN YOU ARE SICK and WILL NOT COME TO WORK FOR YOUR SCHEDULED SHIFT

YOU MUST CALL no less than 2 hours before

your scheduled shift begins: Verbally speak to the ASSISTANT MANAGER and verbally speak to the assistant manager; you will not be coming in to work. You must repeat this same procedure each day you will be unable to come to work. This should provide time to revise the schedule and have coverage.

3. WHEN YOU WANT TIME OFF; NO VACATIONS DAYS PRIOR TO 90 DAYS OF EMPLOYMENT

YOU MUST submit in writing; date it (one) 1 month in advance to the MANAGER only. No two people may take off at the same time! You must receive an approval from the Manager only. The Manager will also document it on your written request and file it. If someone else has requested the same days, the person who submitted the request first may have the time off if it may be arranged due to staffing. (Be sure and date your request).

If you want off just for one day & it was unexpected and less than 2 weeks in advance, you must get another employee/co-worker to work for you.

If you desire to switch shifts with someone you

BOTH must SPEAK to the ASSISTANT MANAGER AND VERBALLY tell them you are switching hours with someone and or they are solely working for you. Due to incidents in the past and as of our staff meeting 01/18/2016, you must also put it in writing WITH BOTH SIGNATURES OF BOTH EMPLOYEES, THE DATE AND TIME OF THE CHANGES and place in the Managers office for final APPROVAL!

4. SWAPPING DAYS: You and the person that is swapping provide a date, who, when and both sign the document (sheet of paper). It must be approved by the Manager only prior to the change!

Policy on Vaccine-Preventable Diseases

ANCHOR WAY SENIOR CARE

All residents are unable to wear a mask due to dementia, confusion, or discomfort.

All staff, visitors, clinical personnel, must wear a mask when inside our facility (optional for your facility).

PL 19-25 (ALL) 4/9/2020 Page 2 of 4 extent the

recommendations are consistent with applicable regulatory requirements for the setting. Providers should adopt, implement, and enforce their policies and procedures, and ensure staff are trained accordingly. The revisions recommend conducting and documenting a TB test, TB risk assessment, and a TB symptom evaluation at hiring as a baseline reference. After an initial screening, annual TB testing for health care personnel is recommended <u>only</u> when there is known TB exposure or ongoing TB transmission at a facility or agency. However, annual TB symptom evaluation is recommended for personnel with untreated latent TB infection and should be considered for certain groups at increased occupational risk for TB exposure or in settings in which TB transmission has occurred in the past. The revisions also recommend annual TB education for health care personnel that includes the following topics: • TB risk factors; • the signs and symptoms of TB disease; and • TB infection control policies and procedures. For more information regarding the revised recommendations, visit the CDC website at: https://www.cdc.gov/tb/topic/testing/healthcare workers.htm. 3.0 Background/History Recent

data has suggested that U.S. healthcare personnel are no longer at an increased risk for TB. Based on this new data, the CDC has revised the recommendations made in its 2005 guidelines related to TB screening, testing, and treatment of health care personnel. This letter notifies providers of the changes so that they can revise their own policies and practices accordingly. PL 19-25 (ALL) 4/9/2020 Page 3

This policy implements ANCHOR WAY SENIOR CARE, LLC procedures on vaccine-preventable diseases, in accordance with Texas regulations/statutes.

This policy specifies the vaccines that an **employee or contractor providing direct resident care** must receive, based on the risk that the employee or contractor presents to residents. (Contractor means an outside entity this facility contracts with to provide direct resident care.)

 The purpose of the policy is to protect the residents of ANCHOR WAY SENIOR CARE from

Vaccine-preventable diseases.

A "covered individual" is defined in regulation/statute as:

an employee of this facility; or

an individual providing direct resident care under a contract with this facility. (Individuals/agencies/entities who contract directly with residents/families are not included.)

Vaccine-preventable diseases are those diseases included in the most current recommendations of the Advisory Committee on Immunization Practices (ACIP) of the Centers for Disease Control and Prevention (CDC).

CDC recommended vaccines include **BUT ARE OPTIONAL**:

Hepatitis B (OPTIONAL)

Influenza (OPTIONAL)

Coronavirus 19 (OPTIONAL)

This facility has determined that certain diseases may pose risks to residents in this facility. [These diseases may be preventable through vaccines.] Accordingly, the following vaccine(s) have been identified, based on the level of risk to residents, as those required for employees who provide direct resident care, unless an exemption is declared: ***(facility may choose not to provide or require these... this is an example; OSHA requires you to offer Hepatitis B)***

Hepatitis B (Optional to Residents and Employees)

Influenza (Optional to Residents and Employees)

Employees providing direct resident care must provide proof to this facility that they are current on the required vaccines or that they declare an exemption.

Current employees must provide documentation in a timely manner to facility management on the required vaccines. Failure to provide the required documentation may result in the employee being taken off the work schedule until the required documentation is submitted.

For new-hires, proof is required within two weeks (14 days) *(not in statute; facility sets time)* of employment. Failure to provide the required documentation may result in the employee being taken off the work schedule until the required documentation is submitted.

This facility will maintain documentation on required vaccines for all facility staff that provide direct resident care.

The CDC lists contraindications to vaccinations for medical conditions. An employee or contractor, who has a medical condition that exempts the employee/contractor from receiving any required vaccine, will make that declaration in writing to facility management. The facility will maintain this information. The facility will not discriminate or retaliate against an employee/contractor exempt under CDC guidelines.

Employees/contractors are responsible for making the determination that he/she may have a medical condition that exempts the employee/contractor from receiving the required vaccines.

An employee who is exempt from the required vaccines must follow facility procedures to protect residents from exposure to disease during a public health disaster or emergency. Facility management will determine the procedures an exempted employee must follow, based on the level of risk the individual presents to residents during the routine and direct exposure to the resident. Those procedures may require the exempted employee to: wear gloves; wear masks;

not provide direct resident care during the emergency/disaster.

This facility does not contract directly with outside entities/agencies to provide direct resident care. Individual residents, resident's Physician and families may contract directly with outside individuals/entities/agencies to provide additional direct care to residents in this facility. The vaccine requirement does not apply to outside contractors providing direct resident care, when the resident and/or family contracts with that entity. If INTERTWINED SENIOR CARE, LLC contracts with an outside entity to provide direct resident care, a copy of this policy will be shared with the outside entities/agencies providing direct care to residents in this facility. The facility will maintain documentation that the entities/agencies have received a copy of this policy. Any facility-contracted entity must adhere to this policy.

POLICY AND PROCEDURE UPDATES: **12/5/2013** (includes prior policy as well)

All staff,

I understand and will follow the "update or reminder" policy and procedures. I understand the past policy and procedures are included.

All bed alarms will be attached and ready for use at all times while residents are in bed.

All residents who wear dentures will be cleaned each night on second shift and rinsed each morning on the first shift.

Give snacks on time 10:00am, 3:00pm and 8:00pm. Follow the snack schedule when items are available.

Manage medications on time....................To the correct individual (look at the picture on the bottle and carefully give medications) avoid distractions. If you are managing medications do not be engaged in any other job duty.

Give PRN medication only after you spoke to management for approval and record as shown in the PRN binder.

Follow the menu daily for each meal.

Serve meals on time; 8am breakfast.............12noon lunch....5pm dinner NO EXCEPTIONS!!

TAKE EVERY RESIDENT TO THE RESTROOM every two (2) hours; or 1 hour for specified residents each shift, **last restroom break should be** 1 hour before you leave. Shift coming to work first 1st restroom break should be 1 hour after you have arrived, then every two (2) hours during your shift.

Leave a lamp on in every room to avoid residents getting up during the night; confused, drowsy due to medications, etc..... to avoid falls............. for management to see the resident's movement/actions in case of emergencies.

Turn off televisions in bedrooms when the resident falls asleep. Keep a lamp on for the residents to see at night.

Stay awake!!! Keep residents safe at all times.

DO NOT BLOCK WINDOWS IN BEDROOMS; If there are two windows, once must be left open for emergency evacuation. If one window, it must be left open for emergency evacuation.

When they are up walking, especially at house #2, you must be close enough to help if they are losing their balance...............break the fall but avoid hurting the resident or yourself.

Observation or incident reports for messages to management or request but complete; **Observation Notes**, when you "SEE" a change, bruise, rash, swelling, etc..... **Incident Report** when the resident falls, needs emergency assistance, causes harm to themselves or another resident.........etc.

Do not wear headscarves or bare feet at work; Come with Anchor Way scrubs and grip safe shoes

Do not change depends (adult underwear) unless it is wet, smells or is soiled. Otherwise, 1st shift will put on a fresh one each morning. If you are taking the residents to the restroom every two hours this should save on the underwear. We are using too many!!!

These are charged to the resident's Medicare bill.

Report to work on time and as scheduled. Your teammate would like to go home on time. You must not be late nor call in during your 90-day probationary period. Post probationary period, you must not be more than 5 minutes late. You must call in 2 hours before your shift begins if you are unable to come to work. After your 90-day probationary period, you may request for time off with the following: In writing, your name, date, day you are requesting off, signature and place under Manager's door. **NOTE**: The date is <u>"not"</u> automatically approved. It may be declined if someone else is off and requested the time before you. However, we will do our best to provide the time off for you if possible and it is after your 90-day probationary period.

Do not text, email, leave a message or fax any request for call-in: being late, off, sick, emergencies or similar. **You must "speak" to the Assistant Manager. If the assistant manager is with a resident, understand she will not answer the phone. CALL BACK! Otherwise, do disrespect but *it will be considered a no call no show and automatic termination.***

Do not leave a resident unattended: to go to your car, to go next door, to go out in the yard, to go

out and smoke is unacceptable; immediate termination. ON GARBAGE DAYS, the shift that is leaving shall take out the garbage cans. The shift coming on shall bring them back in. **AS LONG AS A RESIDENT IS IN THE HOUSE AN ATTENDANT OR MANAGER MUST BE IN THE HOUSE.**

Do not pull a resident up from the bed or chair by their arms!!! EVER. If you need to know how to lift properly let management know. We can assist you or have one of our Home Health or Hospice teammates teach you.

Do not bruise, scratch, bump resident's bodies. Their skin is thin and easy to bruise. Always document.

Do not accept money from a resident nor another employee.

Do not eat nor take residents food, which includes all foods at Anchor Way Senior Care, LLC,

Do not yell at a resident

Do not ignore a resident

Do not serve expired foods, medication or beverages

You may not always agree with the rules and regulations of this facility; always feel free to make suggestions but avoid gossip. No one can tell you why we do what we do better than management. **Please, if you have questions ask me. Monday through Friday 9:00am-5pm 817 297-3426**

Do not discuss the residents AFFAIRS with their families nor other families, direct all questions to the Manager

Please understand these rules are in place for a reason. It has probably happened and caused negative impact on the company, the resident or the employee or all three. Please commit and understand it is not personal, its business.

<u>**A public health emergency**</u> is defined as: *Declaration by the governor of state of disaster; and determination by the Commissioner that there exists an immediate threat from a communicable disease that poses high risk of*

death or serious long-term disability to many people and creates a substandard risk of public exposure because of the disease's high level of contagious or the method by which the disease is transmitted.

In the event of a public health disaster, as defined in statute, this facility may limit access from outside entities/agencies under contract with the facility. During a public health disaster, outside staff providing direct resident care will follow this facility's policies on vaccine-preventable diseases. This includes any procedures for entity/agency staff who claim an exemption from this facility's policies.

Acknowledgement of Responsibility for Reporting Abuse, Neglect and Exploitation and Reasonable Suspicion of Crime

(Form must be completed by the employee, contract employee or volunteer with the original kept at the facility. A copy of each form completed by an employee must be sent to:

HHS Human Resources, Mail Code 1524, 4900 N. Lamar Blvd., Austin, TX 78751-2316)

A. Reporting Abuse, Neglect and Exploitation

All state supported living center employees, contract employees and volunteers must immediately,

if possible, but in no case more than one hour, notify the facility director and the Texas Department of Family and Protective Services if there is suspicion of abuse, neglect or exploitation.

Abuse, neglect and exploitation include, but are not limited to:

1. sexual contact between an individual receiving services and an employee, contractor or volunteer.

2. sexual contact between an individual receiving services and someone who has an ongoing relationship with the individual receiving services, such as a family member or guardian.

3. permitting an obscene or pornographic photograph, videotape or other depiction of an individual receiving services.

4. any intentional or reckless act or failure to act that causes or may have caused physical injury to an individual receiving services.

5. any act of inappropriate or excessive force or corporal punishment inflicted on an individual

receiving

services regardless of whether it results in physical injury.

6. verbally or nonverbally cursing, vilifying, degrading or threatening physical or emotional harm to an

individual receiving services.

7. any act or omission by an employee, contractor or volunteer that places an individual receiving services at risk of physical or emotional injury.

8. using an individual receiving services, or that individual's resources, for monetary or personal benefit, profit or gain. The proper use of restraints and techniques to manage aggressive behavior are not considered abuse or neglect if used according to facility procedures.

I acknowledge my responsibility as an employee, contract employee or volunteer of the state supported living centers to report abuse, neglect and exploitation. I understand that I should report any incident that I suspect may be abuse, neglect or exploitation even if I am not sure. I realize I may be criminally liable for failing to report abuse, neglect or exploitation.

B. Reporting Reasonable Suspicion of Crime against a Resident

All DADS state supported living center employees, contract employees and volunteers must immediately notify the facility director/designee and the DADS Consumer Rights and Services section at 1-800-458-9858 and [name of local law enforcement jurisdiction] at [phone number of jurisdiction] if they have a reasonable suspicion a crime against a resident has occurred. Reporting must occur within 2 hours if the individual sustained a serious physical injury or within 24 hours if the resident did not sustain a serious physical injury I acknowledge my responsibility as an employee, contract employee or volunteer of the state supported living centers to report reasonable suspicion of a crime against a resident. I understand that I should report any incident that I suspect may be a crime even if I am not sure. I realize that if I fail to report as required, I may be subject to civil money penalties and/or barred from participation in any federal health care program.

Date _____

Employee, Contract Employee or Volunteer Name (printed)	Employee Signature

SPECIAL NOTES:

"ALL" VISITORS **MUST** SIGN IN AND OUT

- PLEASE SEE ALL VISITORS TO AND OUT OF THE DOOR WHEN THEY LEAVE

- PLEASE DO NOT REARRANGE THE FURNITURE: it is placed in certain positions for a reason.

- Our television is for the Residents; please do not SELECT CHANNELS because it's your favorite show. Allow them to watch their favorite shows.

- Medications are to be given on time; beginning at 8:00 am PRN means as needed. Please get verbal approval from a manager or Assistant Manager before you give prn medications.

Food Preparation:

Please do not cook foods too hard nor on high, leaving the burners full of spilled foods. THAW AND WASH CHICKEN/MEATS IF APPLICABLE BEFORE COOKING IT. Make your foods attractive and tasty as if you are preparing it for you or your family or a very special guest

Housekeeping

Follow the most current job checklist, especially regarding dusting, sweeping, mopping especially the cleaning the bathrooms, and cleaning of the commodes is not being done consistently. I always expect the house to be clean and sanitized AFTER EACH USE as if a family is coming to visit the home for a potential resident.

• DO NOT GIVE PHONE NUMBERS OF ANY EMPLOYEE OR RESIDENT TO ANYONE. Please take the number, i.e., *IF SOMEONE CALLS FOR A RESIDENT ESPECIALLY IF YOU KNOW IT IS NOT THEIR SON OR DAUGHTER DO NOT VERIFY THAT THEY ARE HERE. OR NOT. CALL Mrs. Woods.*

PERSONAL HYGEINE:

Please come to work with your pressed scrubs on (top and bottom). A clean body smelling fresh is a must. Avoid wearing large earrings or rings. This will minimize skin tears and injury to our residents. Professionalism is important. Please be sure your shoes are clean, and on your feet.

Conserve electricity and water. Do not allow the water to run for long periods of time. The temperature of the hot water heater must be 100 to 120 degrees Fahrenheit. Do not leave lights on that are not needed. Lamps must be on in order for Residents to see during the night.

At night, be sure halls and rooms are well lit especially for residents who can walk or may be confused.

If you are with a Resident do not be concerned with the doorbell or the phone. Safely get the Resident situated, seated, in bed etc....... then answer the doorbell or phone.

Know your own schedule. The only time the schedule may change is if an employee is terminated. If any employee will be off the schedule for long periods of time.

Watch your tone with the residents. No arguing, no demands, no short snappy words, no yelling, no ignoring, no pulling on arms wrist legs aggressively, no grabbing forcefully handling any body parts aggressively. Speak to them at eye level and with a kind verbal tones at all times.

We are not as attentive as we should be with our Residents; **if they move, you move**. This is to avoid falls. The worst thing is for you to call me and say "Mr./Mrs. so and so has fallen". My question to you will be, where were you? What were you doing? Why were they alone? If you move when they move falls should not happen less.

Consistently Assist all residents with toileting; wipe front to back!!! No dried poop should be in the pull-ups.

NOTE: If a family member of our resident or home health or hospice staff is in the building; keep your comments, personal business, side bar chats (what you did last night or your private life) to yourself. Do not discuss another Resident. DO NOT DISCUSS ANOTHER EMPLOYEE. You guys should be a team. A real team does not allow outsiders to come in and tear them apart. Do not discuss a residents' personal affairs, illness, or any other privacy issues with ANYONE. Direct them and all questions to me. They all have my phone numbers.

HOSPICE/HOME HEALTH: They are here to enhance what we do. My advice would be to work with them unless you want to begin giving showers too. I would rather they did. Many of you have had concerns about them and they about you. No one is perfect. All the female hormones in one place are always a big deal. New way of doing things: go to that person and professionally tell them your concerns; communicate. If at that time it is not resolved, bring it to my attention. Many times, we think we are doing a really great job and everyone else need to step it up and do better. The reality is, we have all made errors. AMAZINGLY, none of the complaints have to do with ways to make the RESIDENTS life easier. I hear some amazing stuff. So here goes.

All staff must KNOW THE VISION OF THE OWNER; When determining whether it is safe for your elderly loved one to remain living at home, caregivers cannot let rational decisions take a back seat to emotions. By this I mean, if a resident is coming to your facility, they have needs. They may hit, use profane language, spit, cry, yell.......your staff must be trained to react in a positive caring manner. Realizing, the residents could be in pain, afraid, confused and unable to express it. Be caring, always loving and patient. Never ask why they are acting this way but are you in pain? Do you need me to get something for you? Are you uncomfortable? Do you want to go outside? Do you need to use the restroom. Allow them time to answer you. Perfect segway to the following:

3.3 Termination of Employment (if staff cannot follow instructions as above this may need to occur:

Termination of employment is an inevitable part of personnel activity within any organization, and many of the reasons for termination are routine. Common circumstances under which employment is terminated include the following:

- **Resignation** - Voluntary employment termination initiated by an employee.

- **Termination** - Involuntary employment termination initiated by ANCHOR WAY SENIOR CARE LLC. In most cases, ANCHOR WAY SENIOR CARE LLC will use progressive disciplinary actions before dismissing an employee. However, certain actions warrant immediate termination.

- **Layoff** - Involuntary employment termination initiated by ANCHOR WAY SENIOR CARE LLC for non-disciplinary reasons.

- **Retirement** - Voluntary employee termination upon eligibility for retirement.

Employees who intend to terminate employment with ANCHOR WAY SENIOR CARE LLC, shall provide ANCHOR WAY SENIOR CARE LLC with at least two weeks of written notice. Such notice is intended to allow the Company time to adjust to the employee's departure without placing undue burden on those employees who may be required to fill in before a replacement can be found.

Since employment with ANCHOR WAY SENIOR CARE LLC is based on mutual consent, both the employee and ANCHOR WAY SENIOR CARE LLC have the right to terminate employment at-will, with or without cause, at any time.

In the case of employee termination, the employee will receive their accrued pay in accordance with all federal, state and local laws.

Any employee who terminates employment with ANCHOR WAY SENIOR CARE LLC shall return all files, records, keys, and any other materials that are the property of ANCHOR WAY SENIOR CARE LLC. immediately.

STAFFING

The ratio of staff to residents shall be; THIS NUMBER MAY CHANGE TO 1:8-9 IF CENSUS IS LOW ENOUGH

___2__ : ___16__ during the day shift,

_ 2___ : __16___during the evening and

___2__ : ___16__during the night.

All Employees must be 18 years or older and shall adhere to the following guidelines:

1. Equal Employment Opportunity

Employees are accepted for employment without discrimination based on race, sex, creed, religion, color, national origin, age or handicap. Employees must, however, meet the specific job requirements for the position as outlined in the job descriptions.

2. Probation Period

NOTE: The first ninety (90) days of your employment will be regarded as a period during which both you and the manager can determine your ability to fill your position. Employment will be offered contingent upon a criminal investigation check**. If the criminal investigation check comes back in disfavor, your employment will be terminated immediately.** The manager will discuss and evaluate your work performance with you at intervals during the three (3) months. In the event your evaluation is not satisfactory, you may be terminated at any time without advance notice.

At the end of the ninety (90) day probationary period, if your evaluation and work performance has been satisfactory, you will be given regular employee status. You will be reviewed annually thereafter.

3. Pre-employment Physicals and Health Certification

Each employee will provide documentation of results from TB tests performed. Any employee may be requested by the Manager to have a pre-employment physical examination by a licensed physician at their own expense.

4. Job Descriptions

The duties of each employee are outlined in detail specifying the duties and responsibilities of the position. The Manager has a complete file of all job descriptions and will revise as deemed necessary for good management and operation of the facility. An employee may be given more than one position, meaning that a job description would encompass more than one position or several job descriptions. A job duty checklist will also be provided for you. **<u>Cell phone are not permitted for any reason (emergency calls must be minimal) but is not permitted during work hours, especially while you are with a resident. No sitting around unless you are spending that time with the Residents.</u> NO LAPTOP COMPUTERS AND NO IPADS while on duty. No gossiping. No profane language. You must work while on duty and not stand around talking about things unrelated to the Residents on company time.**

NOTE: All payroll checks are directly deposited into a checking account at a bank only; there are no hand-written checks nor pay card options are available.

2. Work Schedules; Work schedules will be provided and posted by the Manager or Assistant Manager.

3. Absences and Tardiness; SEE EXPLANATION ON PREVIOUS PAGES REGARDING HOW TO HANDLE ATTENDANCE ISSUES. As soon as you find that you will not be on duty because of sickness or for any reason, call the manager immediately. Failure to call in at least two hours in advance may warrant immediate dismissal. ***Repeated OR excessive (3 in one*** *month is excessive) AND (10 in one year is excessive) absenteeism is grounds for dismissal.*

Any employee who has been under the care of a physician for any illness or surgical procedure requiring absence from duty must present a statement from his/her physician giving permission to return to work and any limitations.

All employees are expected to be punctual in reporting to work. Repeated and habitual tardiness will not be tolerated.

Wage and Salary Administration;

1. Time SHEET AND CLOCKING IN; All employees must sign in punctually at the beginning and end of their scheduled shift as well as their lunch break. **All employees are to fill in, total, sign and date their own timesheet according to the dates given in in writing in advance. Time must be completed on the 14th and 29th of each month with time going in for processing on the 18TH th FOR THE FIRST THROUGH THE 15TH AND BY THE LAST working day of each month with time reported on the 3rd for THE 16TH THROUGH 30TH OR 1ST. The only exception is the month of February.**

Excessive tardiness late or absences; (passed 5 minutes is considered late):" o" <u>ZERO</u> during 90-day probationary period.

MAXIMUM OF 10 DAYS off ANNUALLY AFTER YOUR 90 DAY PROBATIONARY PERIOD. This includes sick, off, vacation etc.....

Failure to comply with any of the above regulations may subject an employee to disciplinary action and/or discharge.

2. *Pay Day revised 05/17/2013;* Pay day will be discussed in advance of hire. Direct deposit required. Payroll will be entered on the 15th and last day of each month. You will receive pay via direct deposit within 24-72 hours from the 15th or last working day of the month.

3. *Lunch Period; 30 -minute paid working lunch inside the facility.* Since we are a 24-hour facility you may not leave the premises. Two 5-minute **SMOKE BREAKS** per scheduled shift ALLOWED inside your own vehicle. DO NOT walk about the grounds or street.

General Information; Uniforms required:

1. Personal Appearance/Uniforms

Each employee should WEAR RED SCRUBBS with the Anchor Way Logo with grip shoes. Take a personal interest in being fresh, neat and clean always. Special attention should be given to neat dress, cleans shoes and personal hygiene.

Discreet jewelry may be worn if it is not unsafe and does not interfere with the job. NO LONG NAILS OR GAWDY JEWELRY. Anchor Way Senior Care will provide your first uniform, however

If you are terminated; voluntarily or involuntarily prior (for any reason) to your 90-day probationary period, a $25 uniform fee will be deducted from your last paycheck.

All personnel shall dress in clean attire. The clothing must be clean, in good repair and of appropriate nature for the health care setting. Employees who cook or work in or about the kitchen area will wear hair restraints. Employees while infected with a disease in a communicable form shall not work in the food service area

2. Pregnancy

Pregnancies must be reported as soon as confirmed. A written statement must be obtained from your physician giving permission to continue your duties and noting the approximate date of delivery. *Revised 05/17/2013 If the proper documentation is not received immediately, you will be removed from the schedule.*

3. Ethics and Conduct

All employees are expected to maintain high standards of performance. Kindness and friendliness toward our residents are expected at all times. Abuse or neglect of residents will not be tolerated. Employees will not gossip, make unnecessary noises or engage in other activities that would disturb the residents. Employees are expected to cooperate with their managers and co-workers. Information concerning residents is CONFIDENTIAL and is not to be released to unauthorized persons. Inquiries concerning a resident's condition or personal affairs should be referred to the manager.

Qualification

Direct care staff must "not" include:

1. Persons who are mentally, physically or

emotionally unable to perform assigned duties.

2. Persons whose behavior or health appears to endanger the health, safety and well-being of the residents.

3. Persons unable to read and write English.

4. Have Limitations to what hours they can and cannot work; not flexible

5. Gossip

Personnel Records

A separate file is maintained on each employee. This file will contain the following:

1. Application for employment

2. Verification of Criminal Investigation Check

3. Verification of I-9 information.

4. Record of training and orientation to facility.

5. Evaluations of work performance.

6. Written reprimands, when given, for failure to follow facility policies.

7. Verification that employee has completed an educational course about Human Immunodeficiency Virus Infection.

8. Verification that attendants have the following knowledge prior to assuming responsibilities:

    a. needs of the residents

    b. tasks to be provided

    c. resident's health conditions and how it affects provision of tasks

    d. conditions about which the attendant should routinely notify the facility manager.

Staff Training Program

New employees must complete four hours of orientation prior to assuming any job responsibilities in the following areas:

Reporting of abuse and neglect

Confidentiality of resident information

Universal Precautions

Conditions about which they should notify the facility manager

Residents' Rights

Emergency and evacuation procedures

New employees must complete 16 hours of on-the-job supervision and training within the first 16 hours of employment following orientation in the following areas:

Aiding with the activities of daily living

Resident's health conditions and how they may

affect provision of tasks

Safety measures to prevent accidents and injuries

Emergency first aid procedures, such as the Heimlich maneuver and actions to take when a resident fall, suffers a laceration, or experiences a sudden change in physical and/or mental status

Managing dysfunctional behavior

Direct care staff must complete six documented hours of education annually based on each employee's hire date. Licensed nurses, nurse aides or medication aides must receive in-service annually, appropriate to their job responsibilities.

Health Screening (IMPORTANT)

All personnel must have a onetime TB screening before 14 days of hire date as one time unless there is reason to suspect exposure to TB.

Long-Term Care Regulatory Provider Letter Number: PL 20-25 Title: Revised Recommendations for Tuberculosis Screening, Testing, and Treatment of Health Care Personnel Provider Types: Assisted Living Facility, Day Activity and Health Services Facility, Intermediate Care Facility for Individuals with an Intellectual

Disability or Related Conditions, Home and
Community Support Services Agency, Nursing
Facility, and Prescribed Pediatric Extended Care
Center Date Issued: April 09, 2020 1.0 Subject and
Purpose The Texas Health and Human Services
Commission (HHSC) is issuing this letter to
inform providers that the Center for Disease
Control and Prevention (CDC) has made changes
to its 2005 guidelines related to tuberculosis (TB)
screening, testing, and treatment of health care
personnel. Specifically, on May 17, 2019, the CDC
and the National TB Controllers Association
(NTCA) released from those in the 2005 CDC
"Guidelines for Preventing the Transmission of
Mycobacterium tuberculosis in Health-Care
Settings." The revisions add a recommendation
that pre-placement TB screening of all U.S. health
care personnel include an individual TB risk
assessment. In addition, annual TB testing for
health care personnel is no longer recommended
unless there is known TB exposure or ongoing
transmission of TB in the setting. The revised
recommendations also encourage treatment for all
health care personnel with latent TB infection. The
revisions are summarized in the table on page 4 of
this letter. 2.0 Provider Responsibilities & Policy
Details LTCR providers should review their

infection prevention and control policies and practices and align them with the revised recommendations, to the PL 19-25 (ALL) 4/9/2020 Page 2 of 4 extent the recommendations are consistent with applicable regulatory requirements for the setting. Providers should adopt, implement, and enforce their policies and procedures, and ensure staff are trained accordingly. The revisions recommend conducting and documenting a TB test, TB risk assessment, and a TB symptom evaluation at hiring as a baseline reference. After an initial screening, annual TB testing for health care personnel is recommended only when there is known TB exposure or ongoing TB transmission at a facility or agency. However, annual TB symptom evaluation is recommended for personnel with untreated latent TB infection and should be considered for certain groups at increased occupational risk for TB exposure or in settings in which TB transmission has occurred in the past. The revisions also recommend annual TB education for health care personnel that includes the following topics: • TB risk factors; • the signs and symptoms of TB disease; and • TB infection control policies and procedures. For more information regarding the revised recommendations, visit the CDC website at:

https://www.cdc.gov/tb/topic/testing/healthcarewor kers.htm. 3.0 Background/History Recent data has suggested that U.S. healthcare personnel are no longer at an increased risk for TB. Based on this new data, the CDC has revised the recommendations made in its 2005 guidelines related to TB screening, testing, and treatment of health care personnel. This letter notifies providers of the changes so that they can revise their own policies and practices accordingly. PL 19-25 (ALL) 4/9/2020 Page 3 of 4 4.0 Contact Information If you have any questions about this letter, please contact the Policy, Rules and Training Section by email at PolicyRulesTraining@hhsc.state.tx.us or call (512) 438-3161

The kind of employees you may want to avoid are as follows:

*****Excessive leaning and/or sitting while on the shift.**

- **Gross insubordination**
- **Drug or alcohol use on premises**
- **Neglect (suspected or factual/proven)**

 abuse: verbal or physical of Resident or failure to report abuse or neglect;

- <u>**SLEEPING WHILE ON DUTY!**</u> <u>**(03/19/2013).**</u>
- **Failure to report to work without notification; NO CALL- NO SHOW or having someone call in for you. YOU MUST CALL IN YOURSELF.**
- **Any criminal act, ESPECIALLY THEFT, eating resident food, taking resident cash.... weapons, molestation, touching inappropriately, inappropriate verbal language.**
- **UPDATE change of verbiage *******(Anchor Way Staff) ******<u>Leaving resident unattended at any time for any reason; EVER! AN ANCHOR WAY staff member must be in the facility at all times. Especially if a resident is in the facility</u>*********

REVISED 01/18/2013: <u>**Especially if you have caused an unnecessary/undo fall, bruises, and or injury to a Resident.**</u>

- **Negative attitude problems which could potentially affect the safety and well-being of residents/employees**
- **90 days: "o" <u>ZERO</u> days late or absent during 90-day probationary period. A**

MAXIMUM 5 times calling in approved absences ANNUALLY. YOU MUST PROVIDE A PHYSICIANS NOTE FOR PROOF OF ABSENCE. MAXIMUM OF 5 times late ANNUALLY. No exceptions. This includes habitual reasons such as I have no way to get to work, I have no gas, I do not have a ride, I did not get my paycheck yet; these are <u>unexcused absences</u> and not a reason to miss work. All other reasons will be evaluated case by case, but all staff will be treated the same.

- <u>Failure to follow instructions given by management, verbal or written.</u>
- <u>Failure to provide proof of TB test within 14 business days one time upon hire.</u>
- The use of cell phones & computers of any type are NOT allowed during your shift. If an injury TO A RESIDENT is caused, immediate termination <u>will</u> occur.
- If you are resigning and fail to provide a WRITTEN two-week notice (courtesy) to the manager (text, emails, nor voice mails are not acceptable) immediate termination will occur.

> ➤ **GOSSIP!!!! and WORTHLESS drama among your peers; this promotes neglecting the care of the residents and too much wasted time. We are servicing the elderly. An incident could happen in seconds. Always be attentive and quick to respond to the needs of our residents without distractions.**

ANCHOR WAY SENIOR CARE LLC provide elder care twenty-four-seven. However, office hours are: Monday - Friday 9:00 AM to 5:00 PM

This excludes holidays recognized by **ANCHOR WAY SENIOR CARE LLC**. The standard workweek is 40 hours.

Supervisors will advise employees of their scheduled shift, including starting and ending times. Business needs may necessitate a variation in your starting and ending times as well as in the total hours you may be scheduled to work each day and each week.

4.2 Safety

ANCHOR WAY SENIOR CARE LLC is committed to providing a clean, safe, and healthful work environment for its employees. Maintaining a safe work environment, however, requires the continuous cooperation of all employees.

ANCHOR WAY SENIOR CARE LLC and all employees must comply with all occupational safety and health standards and regulations established by the Occupational Safety and Health Act and state and local regulations. In addition, all employees are expected to obey safety rules and exercise caution and common sense in all work activities.

Employees must immediately report any unsafe conditions to their supervisor. Employees who violate safety standards, cause hazardous or dangerous situations, or fail to report or, where appropriate, remedy such situations may be subject to disciplinary action, up to and including termination of employment.

In the case of an accident that results in injury, regardless of how seemingly insignificant the injury may appear, employees must notify their supervisor.

Questions regarding this policy should be directed to your supervisor or the MANAGER.

4.3 Meal & Break Periods

In accordance with state and local laws, non-exempt employees will be provided with a 30-minute working (paid) lunch. NEVER EAT A RESIDENT'S FOODS/drinks.

4.4 Break Time for Nursing Mothers

ANCHOR WAY SENIOR CARE
LLC accommodates employees who wish to express breast milk during the workday by providing reasonable break times to do so.
The Company will provide a designated room, other than a bathroom, that is shielded from view, free from intrusion from coworkers and the public and is in compliance with all other applicable laws for this purpose.

Employees who use regularly scheduled rest breaks to express breast milk will be paid for the break time. If the lactation break does not run concurrently with the employees regularly scheduled compensated break, the lactation break time will be unpaid.

For questions related to this policy, please contact

the MANAGER.

4.5 Security

The purpose of ANCHOR WAY SENIOR CARE LLC's security policy is to protect Company assets and to maintain a safe working environment for all employees and residents.

5.1 Jury Duty

ANCHOR WAY SENIOR CARE LLC encourages employees to fulfill their civic responsibilities when called upon to serve as a juror. Employees must provide their immediate supervisor with a copy of their jury summons as soon as possible so that the supervisor may decide to accommodate their absence.

Employees on jury duty must report to work on workdays, or parts of workdays, when they are not required to serve. Either ANCHOR WAY SENIOR CARE LLC or the employee may request an excuse from jury duty if it is determined that the employee's absence would create serious operational difficulties.

Jury duty will be paid if required by applicable state law. If paid, jury duty pay will be calculated on the employee's base pay rate times the number of hours the employee would otherwise have worked on the day of absence.

5.2 Voting Leave (Texas Employees)

ANCHOR WAY SENIOR CARE LLC requests that, whenever possible, employees vote before or after work hours to avoid interference with business operations. However, if an employee does not have sufficient time outside of work hours to cast his or her ballot, the employee may be eligible for time off to vote.

ANCHOR WAY SENIOR CARE LLC may specify the hours during which the employee may take leave to vote. Such time will generally be limited to the beginning or end of a working shift unless otherwise mutually agreed.

If there are fewer than two consecutive hours between the opening of the polls and the beginning of an employee's workday or between the end of an employee's workday and the closing of the polls, an employee may take a reasonable amount of paid leave to vote on Election Day. To the extent possible, employees must provide reasonable notice of their need for leave under this policy.

Employees must be prepared to provide ANCHOR WAY SENIOR CARE LLC with certification, such as a voter's receipt, to prove that he or she voted.

5.3 Military Leave

ANCHOR WAY SENIOR CARE LLC proudly grants employees time off work for service in the uniformed services in accordance with the Uniformed Services Employment and Reemployment Rights Act (USERRA).

All employees requesting time off for military service must provide advance notice of military service to their immediate supervisor, unless military necessity prevents such notice, or it is otherwise impossible or unreasonable.

Continuation of health insurance benefits is available during military leave subject to the terms and conditions of the group health plan and applicable law.

Employees are eligible for re-employment for up to five (5) years from the date their military leave began. The period an individual has to make application for reemployment or report back to work after military service is based on time spent on military duty. For service of less than 31 days, the service member must return at the beginning of the next regularly scheduled work period on the first full day after release from service, considering safe travel home plus an eight-hour rest period. For service of more than 30 days but less than 181 days, the service member must apply for reemployment within 14 days of release from service. For service of more than 180 days, an application for reemployment must be submitted within 90 days of release from service.

Employees who qualify for re-employment will return to active employment at a pay level and status equal to that which they would have attained had they not entered military service. They will be treated as though they were continuously employed for purposes of determining benefits based on length of service.

Questions regarding this policy should be directed to the MANAGER.

5.4 Retirement: Following your 1-year anniversary, you may invest in ANCHOR WAY SENIOR CARE 401k. ANCHOR WAY SENIOR CARE will match up to 4% of your contribution.

6. Employee Conduct

6.1 Standards of Conduct

ANCHOR WAY SENIOR CARE LLC's rules and standards of conduct are essential to our productive work environment. All employees must familiarize themselves with company rules and standards; all employees will be held to them. Any employee who disregards or deviates from company rules or standards may be subject to disciplinary action, up to and including termination of employment.

While not intended to be an all-inclusive list, the examples below represent behavior that is considered unacceptable in the workplace. Behaviors such as these, as well as other forms of misconduct, may result in disciplinary action, up to and including termination of employment:

- Theft or inappropriate removal/possession of property
- Falsification of timekeeping records
- Possession, distribution, sale, transfer, or use of alcohol or illicit drugs in the workplace
- Fighting or threatening violence in the workplace
- Gossiping or spreading rumors about co-workers
- Boisterous or disruptive activity in the workplace
- Negligence or improper conduct leading to damage of company-owned or customer-owned property
- **Excessive tardiness or absenteeism or any absence with or without notice**
- Violation of safety or health rules

- Smoking in the workplace
- Sexual or other unlawful or unwelcome harassment
- **Excessive tardiness or absenteeism or any absence with or without notice**
- Unauthorized use of telephones, computers, or other company-owned equipment
- Unauthorized disclosure of any confidential information

Other forms of misconduct not listed above may also result in disciplinary action, up to and including termination of employment. If you have questions regarding ANCHOR WAY SENIOR CARE LLC's standards of conduct, please direct them to your supervisor.

6.2 Disciplinary Action

Disciplinary action at ANCHOR WAY SENIOR CARE LLC is intended to fairly and impartially correct behavior and performance problems early on and to prevent reoccurrence.

Disciplinary action may involve any of the following: verbal warning, written warning, suspension with or without pay, and termination of employment, depending on the severity of the

problem and the frequency of occurrence.
ANCHOR WAY SENIOR CARE LLC reserves
the right to administer disciplinary action at its
discretion and based upon the circumstances.

ANCHOR WAY SENIOR CARE LLC
recognizes that certain types of employee behavior
are serious enough to justify termination of
employment, without observing other disciplinary
action first.

These violations include but are not limited to:

- Workplace violence
- Harassment
- Theft of any kind
- Insubordinate behavior
- Vandalism or destruction of company property
- Presence on company property during non-business hours
- Use of company equipment and/or company vehicles without prior authorization
- Indiscretion regarding personal work history, skills, or training

- Divulging ANCHOR WAY SENIOR CARE LLC business practices or any other confidential information

• Any misrepresentation of ANCHOR WAY SENIOR CARE LLC to a customer, a prospective customer, the general public, or an employee

6.3 Confidentiality

ANCHOR WAY SENIOR CARE LLC takes the protection of confidential business information and trade secrets very seriously. To protect such information, employees may not disclose any confidential or proprietary information about the Company to any unauthorized individual.

Confidential Information

"Confidential Information" includes, but is not limited to, computer processes, computer programs and codes, customer lists, customer preferences and personal information, company financial data, marketing strategies, proprietary production processes, research and development strategies, pricing information, business and marketing plans, vendor information, software, databases, and information concerning the creation, acquisition or disposition of products and services.

Confidential Information also includes any

information considered to be the intellectual property of the Company. Intellectual property includes, but is not limited to, trade secrets, ideas, discoveries, writings, trademarks, and inventions developed through the course of your employment with ANCHOR WAY SENIOR CARE LLC and as a direct result of your job responsibilities with ANCHOR WAY SENIOR CARE LLC.

Wages and other conditions of employment are not considered to be Confidential Information. Employees are free to discuss these issues with co-workers or third parties for the purpose of improving work conditions.

Inadvertent Disclosure

The unintentional disclosure of Confidential Information can be just as harmful as intentional disclosure. To avoid this, never discuss with any unauthorized person any Confidential Information you may have about the Company. You should never discuss Confidential Information, even with authorized employees, if you are in the presence of others who are not authorized.

If you receive a request for Confidential Information, you should immediately refer the request to your supervisor. If you leave the

Company, you may not disclose or misuse any Confidential Information.

The unauthorized disclosure of Confidential Information belonging to the Company may subject you to disciplinary action, up to and including termination of employment.

Questions regarding this policy should be directed to the MANAGER.

6.4 Personal Appearance

The purpose of ANCHOR WAY SENIOR CARE LLC's personal appearance policy is to ensure a safe and sanitary workplace for all employees. ANCHOR WAY SENIOR CARE LLC strives to maintain a professional working environment that promotes efficiency, positive employee morale and promotes a professional image. During business hours or when representing ANCHOR WAY SENIOR CARE LLC, employees are expected to use common sense and good judgment in order to meet the goals of this policy.

Generally, employees should wear appropriate clothing, observe high standards of personal hygiene, and dress and groom themselves according to the requirements of their positions. While not intended to be an all-inclusive list, the examples below are considered appropriate workplace attire:

Only company approved uniforms

If management designates "casual days," an employee's casual dress must still be clean, neat and project a professional image.

Generally, employees should maintain a clean and neat appearance and should refrain from wearing stained, wrinkled, frayed, or revealing clothing to the workplace. Employees are urged to use their discretion when determining what is appropriate to wear to work. Employees who wear inappropriate attire to work may be sent home to change their clothing.

ANCHOR WAY SENIOR CARE
LLC understands that in certain situations, the Company may need to make exceptions to this policy based on an employee's religion, disability, or other characteristic protected under federal, state or local law. In accordance with all applicable laws, the Company will make every effort to provide reasonable accommodation to the

employee requesting accommodation unless doing so would cause an undue hardship on **ANCHOR WAY SENIOR CARE LLC**.

Questions regarding appropriate workplace attire should be directed to your supervisor or the MANAGER.

6.5 Workplace Violence

ANCHOR WAY SENIOR CARE LLC strictly prohibits workplace violence, including any act of intimidation, threat, harassment, physical violence, verbal abuse, aggression or coercion against a coworker, vendor, customer, or visitor.

Prohibited actions, include, but are not limited to the following examples:

- Physically injuring another person or resident
- Threatening to injure another person or resident
- Engaging in behavior that subjects another person/resident to emotional distress
- Using obscene, abusive or threatening language or gestures
- Bringing an unauthorized firearm or other weapon onto company property

- Threatening to use or using a weapon while on company premises, on company-related business, or during job-related functions
- Intentionally damaging property

All threats or acts of violence should be reported immediately to your supervisor or security personnel. Employees should warn their supervisors or security personnel of any suspicious workplace activity that they observe or that appears problematic. Employee reports made pursuant to this policy will be kept confidential to the maximum extent possible. ANCHOR WAY SENIOR CARE LLC will not tolerate any form of retaliation against any employee for making a report under this policy.

ANCHOR WAY SENIOR CARE LLC will take prompt remedial action, up to calling the police and including immediate termination, against any employee found to have engaged in threatening behavior or acts of violence.

6.6 Drug & Alcohol Use

ANCHOR WAY SENIOR CARE LLC is

committed to maintaining a workplace free of substance abuse. No employee is allowed to consume, possess, sell, purchase, or be under the influence of alcohol or illegal drugs, as defined by federal law, on any property owned by or leased on behalf of ANCHOR WAY SENIOR CARE LLC, or in any vehicle owned or leased on behalf of **ANCHOR WAY SENIOR CARE LLC**.

The use of over-the-counter drugs and legally prescribed drugs is permitted if they are used in the manner for which they were prescribed and provided that such use does not hinder an employee's ability to safely perform his or her job. Employees should inform their supervisor if they believe their medication will impair their job performance, safety or the safety of others, or if they believe they need a reasonable accommodation when using such medication.

ANCHOR WAY SENIOR CARE LLC will not tolerate employees who report for duty while impaired using alcohol or drugs. All employees should report evidence of alcohol or drug abuse to their supervisor or the MANAGER immediately. In cases in which the use of alcohol or drugs creates an imminent threat to the safety of persons or property, employees are required to report the violation. Failure to do so may result in disciplinary action, up to and including termination of employment.

As a part of our effort to maintain a workplace free of substance abuse, **ANCHOR WAY SENIOR CARE LLC** employees may be asked to take a random drug test for the presence of alcohol and/or drugs. Within the limits of federal, state, and local laws, ANCHOR WAY SENIOR CARE LLC reserves the right to examine and test for drugs and alcohol at our discretion.

As a condition of your employment with **ANCHOR WAY SENIOR CARE LLC**, employees must comply with this Drug & Alcohol Use Policy. Be advised that no part of the Drug & Alcohol Use Policy shall be construed to alter or amend the at-will employment relationship between **ANCHOR WAY SENIOR CARE LLC** and its employees.

Employees found in violation of this policy may be subject to disciplinary action, up to and including termination of employment.

6.7 Sexual & Other Unlawful Harassment

ANCHOR WAY SENIOR CARE LLC is committed to a work environment in which all individuals are treated with respect. **ANCHOR WAY SENIOR CARE LLC** expressly prohibits discrimination and all forms of employee harassment based on race, color, religion, sex, national origin, age, disability, military or veteran status, or status in any group protected by state or local law.

Sexual harassment is a form of discrimination and is prohibited by law. For purposes of this policy sexual harassment is defined as unwelcome sexual advances, requests for sexual favors, and other verbal or physical conduct of a sexual nature when this conduct explicitly or implicitly affects an individual's employment, unreasonably interferes with an individual's work performance, or creates an intimidating, hostile, or offensive work environment. Unwelcome sexual advances (either verbal or physical), requests for sexual favors, and other verbal or physical conduct of a sexual nature constitute sexual harassment when: (1) submission to such conduct is made either explicitly or implicitly a term or condition of employment; (2) submission or rejection of the conduct is used as a basis for making employment decisions; or, (3) the conduct has the purpose or effect of interfering with work performance or creating an intimidating, hostile, or offensive work environment.

Sexual and unlawful harassment may include a range of behaviors and may involve individuals of the same or different gender. These behaviors include, but are not limited to:

- Unwanted sexual advances or requests for sexual favors.
- Sexual or derogatory jokes, comments, or innuendo
- Unwelcomed physical interaction
- Insulting or obscene comments or gestures
- Offensive email, voicemail, or text messages
- Suggestive or sexually explicit posters, calendars, photographs, graffiti, or cartoons
- Making or threatening reprisals after a negative response to sexual advances
- Visual conduct that includes leering, making sexual gestures, or displaying of sexually suggestive objects or pictures, cartoons or posters
- Verbal sexual advances or propositions

- Physical conduct that includes touching, assaulting, or impeding or blocking movements

- Abusive or malicious conduct that a reasonable person would find hostile, offensive, and unrelated to the Company's legitimate business interests

- Any other visual, verbal, or physical conduct or behavior deemed inappropriate by the Company

Harassment based on any other protected characteristic is also strictly prohibited.

Complaint Procedure:

ANCHOR WAY SENIOR CARE LLC strongly encourages the reporting of all instances of discrimination, harassment, or retaliation. If you believe you have experienced or witnessed harassment or discrimination based on sex, race, national origin, disability, or another factor, promptly report the incident to your supervisor. If you believe it would be inappropriate to discuss the matter with your supervisor, you may bypass your supervisor and report it directly to:

Owner/manager's name

Address

Phone

Any reported allegations of harassment or discrimination will be investigated promptly, thoroughly, and impartially.

Any employee found to be engaged in any form of sexual or other unlawful harassment may be subject to disciplinary action, up to and including termination of employment.

Retaliation Prohibited:

ANCHOR WAY SENIOR CARE LLC expressly prohibits retaliation against any individual who reports discrimination or harassment or assists in investigating such charges. Any form of retaliation is considered a direct violation of this policy and, like discrimination or harassment itself, will be subject to disciplinary action, up to and including termination of employment.

6.8 Telephone Usage

ANCHOR WAY SENIOR CARE LLC telephones are intended for the sole use of conducting company business. <u>Personal use of the Company's telephones and individually owned cell phones during business hours is prohibited except in emergencies</u>. In addition, long distance phone calls which are not strictly business-related are expressly prohibited.

Any employee found in violation of this policy will be subject to disciplinary action, up to and including termination of employment.

6.9 Personal Property

Employees should use their discretion when bringing personal property into the workplace. **ANCHOR WAY SENIOR CARE LLC** assumes <u>no risk</u> for any loss or damage to personal property. Additionally, employees may not possess or display any property that may be viewed as inappropriate or offensive on **ANCHOR WAY SENIOR CARE LLC** premises.

DO NOT BORROW MONEY FROM ANOTHER EMPLOYEE NOR RESIDENT NOR RESIDENT'S FAMILY!

6.10 Use of Company Property

Company property refers to anything owned by the company: physical, electronic, intellectual, or otherwise. The use of company property is for business necessity only.

When materials or equipment are assigned to an employee for business, it is the employee's responsibility to see that the equipment is used properly and cared for properly. However, always, equipment assigned to the employee remains the property of the Company and is subject to reassignment and/or use by the Company without prior notice or approval of the employee. This includes, but is not limited to, computer equipment and data stored thereon, voicemail, records, and employee files.

ANCHOR WAY SENIOR CARE LLC has created specific guidelines regarding the use of company equipment. Below is a list of employee responsibilities and limitations with regards to company property.

Personal use of company property:

Company property is <u>not</u> permitted to be taken from the premises without proper written authority from company management.

Company Tools:

All necessary tools are furnished to employees in order to assist them in their required duties. Each employee is, in turn, responsible for these tools. Tools damaged or stolen as a result of an employee's negligence will, to the extent permitted by federal, state and local law, be charged to the employee.

Care of Company Property:

Office areas should be kept neat and orderly, and all equipment should be well-maintained. The theft, misappropriation, or unauthorized removal, possession, or use of company property or equipment is expressly prohibited.

Any action in contradiction to the guidelines set herein may result in disciplinary action, up to and including termination of employment.

6.11 Smoking

ANCHOR WAY SENIOR CARE LLC provides a smoke-free environment for its employees, customers, and visitors. Smoking is prohibited throughout the workplace. We have adopted this policy because we have a sincere interest in the health of our employees and in maintaining pleasant working conditions.

SMOKE AT YOUR OWN RISK 2 TIMES FOR 5 MINUTES IN YOUR OWN PERSONAL AUTOMOBILE PER SCHEDULED SHIFT, NOT STANDING AROUND THE PROPERTY NOR NEAR THE PROPANE TANK NOR ON THE GRASS.

6.12 Visitors in the Workplace

To ensure the safety and security of **ANCHOR WAY SENIOR CARE LLC** and its employee's, only authorized visitors are permitted on Company premises and in Company facilities, Home Health, Hospice, Physicians, approved family members, emergency staff, medical equipment companies.

All visitors must enter through the main entry area and sign in and out at the entry way. Authorized visitors will be escorted to their destination. Unauthorized visitors will be escorted out of the building. PLEASE DO NOT BRING YOUR FRIENDS, YOUR CHILDREN NOR SPOUSES TO WORK WITH YOU.

6.13 Computer, Email & Internet Usage

ANCHOR WAY SENIOR CARE LLC's computer systems allow us to be more productive but can cause problems if used improperly. It is extremely important that all employees use good business judgment when using the computer systems.

Computer hardware, software, electronic mail, Internet connections, and all other computer or electronic communication or data storage systems used by **ANCHOR WAY SENIOR CARE LLC** are the property of ANCHOR WAY SENIOR CARE LLC. Employees have no right of personal privacy in their use of ANCHOR WAY SENIOR CARE LLC's computer and electronic communication systems.

To ensure compliance with this policy and all applicable laws, computer, email and Internet usage may be monitored, including but not limited to, reviewing documents created and stored on

ANCHOR WAY SENIOR CARE LLC's computer and electronic communication systems, monitoring sites visited by employees on the Internet, reviewing materials downloaded or uploaded by employees from or to the Internet, and reviewing emails sent and received by employees.

ANCHOR WAY SENIOR CARE LLC strives to maintain a workplace free of harassment and is sensitive to the diversity of its employees. Therefore, **ANCHOR WAY SENIOR CARE LLC** prohibits the use of computers and the email system for bullying, harassing, discriminating, or other unlawful misconduct.

ANCHOR WAY SENIOR CARE LLC purchases and licenses the use of various computer software for business purposes and does not own the copyright to this software or its related documentation. Unless authorized by the software developer, **ANCHOR WAY SENIOR CARE LLC** does not have the right to reproduce such software for use on more than one computer. Employees may only use software according to the software license agreement. **ANCHOR WAY SENIOR CARE LLC** prohibits the illegal duplication of software and its related documentation.

The unauthorized use, installation, copying, or distribution of copyrighted, trademarked, or patented material on the Internet is expressly prohibited. As a rule, if an employee did not create material, does not own the rights to it, or has not gotten authorization for its use, it should not be put on the Internet. Employees are also responsible for ensuring that the person sending any material over the Internet has the appropriate distribution rights. Abuse of this policy may result in disciplinary action, up to and including termination of employment. The following behaviors are examples of previously stated or additional actions and activities that are prohibited and can result in disciplinary action:

- Sending or posting discriminatory, harassing, or threatening messages or images
- Stealing, using, or disclosing someone else's code or password without authorization
- Copying, pirating, or downloading software and electronic files without permission

- Sending or posting confidential material, trade secrets, or proprietary information outside of the organization. Wages and other conditions of employment are not considered to be confidential material.

- Violating copyright law

- Failing to observe licensing agreements

- Engaging in unauthorized transactions that may incur a cost to the organization or initiate unwanted Internet services and transmissions

- Participating in the viewing or exchange of pornography or obscene materials

- Sending or posting messages that defame or slander other individuals

- Attempting to break into the computer system of another organization or person

- Refusing to cooperate with a security investigation

- Using the Internet for gambling or any illegal activities

- Sending or posting messages that disparage another organization's products or services

- Passing off personal views as representing those of **ANCHOR WAY SENIOR CARE LLC**

This policy is not intended to restrict employees' rights to act together to improve wages and other conditions of employment.

Employees should notify their immediate supervisor or any member of management upon learning of violations of this policy.

6.14 Company Supplies

Only authorized persons may purchase supplies in the name of **ANCHOR WAY SENIOR CARE LLC**. No employee whose regular duties do not include purchasing shall incur any expense on behalf of **ANCHOR WAY SENIOR CARE LLC** or bind **ANCHOR WAY SENIOR CARE LLC** by any promise or representation without express written approval.

6.14b My Company Pledge
I PLEDGE TO ALWAYS EXEMPLFY PROFESSIONAL BEHAVIOR AT ALL TIMES WHILE EMPLOYED AT ANCHOR WAY SENIOR CARE; trusted to care for the residents with passion and patience.
WATCHFUL, APPROACHABLE, FRIENDLY,

HELPFUL, POSITIVE, CHEERFUL, AND ATTENTIVE to all residents and resident families always. I PLEDGE TO REMAIN FREE OF VALID RESIDENT AND RESIDENT FAMILY COMPLAINTS. IF AT ANYTIME these characteristics are not met, I understand the possibility of immediate discipline or termination.

6.15 ALZHEIMER/DEMENTIA TRAINING 05/01/2019

(a) A facility must adopt, implement, and enforce a written policy that:

(1) requires a facility employee who provides direct care to a resident with Alzheimer's disease or a related disorder to successfully complete training in the provision of care to residents with Alzheimer's disease and related disorders; and

(2) ensures the care and services provided by a facility employee to a resident with Alzheimer's disease or a related disorder meet the specific identified needs of the resident relating to the diagnosis of Alzheimer's disease or a related disorder.

(b) The training required for facility employees under subsection (a)(1) of this section must include information about:

(1) symptoms of dementia;

(2) stages of Alzheimer's disease;

(3) person-centered behavioral interventions; and

(4) communication with a resident with Alzheimer's disease or a related disorder.

ALZHEIMER/DEMENTIA POLICY
05/01/2019

(a) ANCHOR WAY SENIOR CARE adopts, implement, and enforce a written policy that:

(1) requires a facility employee who provides direct care to a resident with Alzheimer's disease or a related disorder to successfully complete training in the provision of care to residents with Alzheimer's disease and related disorders; and

(2) ensures the care and services provided by a facility employee to a resident with Alzheimer's disease or a related disorder meet the specific identified needs of the resident relating to the diagnosis of Alzheimer's disease or a related disorder.

(b) The training required during the first 16 hours of employment at ANCHOR WAY SENIOR CARE. Employees under subsection (a)(1) of this section must include information about:

(1) symptoms of dementia;

(2) stages of Alzheimer's disease;

(3) person-centered behavioral interventions; and

(4) communication with a resident with Alzheimer's disease or a related disorder.

7.4 Payroll Deductions

Paychecks stubs will not, under any circumstances,

be given to any person other than the employee. Stubs may also be mailed to the employee's listed address or, upon advance written authorization, deposited directly into an employee's bank account. Employees who elect payment through direct deposit will receive an itemized statement of wages when the Company makes direct deposits. In the event of employee termination, the employee will receive their accrued pay in accordance with applicable federal, state and local laws if the employer has the direct deposit information. ANCHOR WAY SENIOR CARE LLC makes deductions from employee pay only in circumstances permitted by applicable law. This includes, but is not limited to, mandatory deductions for income tax withholding and Social Security and Medicare contributions as well as voluntary deductions for health insurance premiums and other related contributions. If you believe that an improper deduction has been made from your pay, raise the issue with the MANAGER immediately. ANCHOR WAY SENIOR CARE LLC will promptly investigate. If the investigation reveals that you were subjected to an improper deduction from pay, you will be reimbursed promptly.

ANCHOR WAY SENIOR CARE RESIDENTS

- *All residents need lots of water each meal and throughout the day.*
- *At least 3 hours of activities daily*
- *All female residents put on a t-shirt, bra, or camisole, and socks each morning.*
- *Treat all residents with respect; verbally, physically and mentally.*
- *Oral care in the mornings and at bedtime with a toothbrush, tooth paste and mouthwash if they can do so.*
- *Hair care daily*

(This list of residents is not given to each family member. This portion is used solely for our EMERGENCY PREPAREDNESS PLAN

Moving to a nursing home can mean giving up many things — your home, your independence and possibly even treasured possessions or pets. One thing people who move to nursing homes do not have to give up is their rights as Texans and Americans.

Residents' Rights Month is observed in October to remind us that moving to a nursing home does not mean giving up your right to dignity and respect. This year's theme "Speak Out Against Elder Abuse!" was selected to call attention to elder abuse and encourage residents, family, friends, advocates, and others to speak out against it.

What is elder abuse?

Elder abuse refers to any knowing, intentional or negligent act by a caregiver or any other person that causes harm or a serious risk of harm to a vulnerable adult (Administration for Community Living). Legislatures in all 50 states have passed some form of elder abuse prevention laws. Broadly defined, abuse may be:

- **Physical**— inflicting physical pain or injury on a senior, e.g., slapping, bruising or restraining by physical or chemical means
- **Sexual**— non-consensual sexual contact of any kind
- **Neglect** — the failure by those responsible to provide food, shelter, health care or protection for a vulnerable elder
- **Exploitation** — the illegal taking, misuse or concealment of funds, property or assets of a senior for someone else's benefit
- **Emotional**— inflicting mental pain, anguish or distress on an elder person through verbal or nonverbal acts, e.g., humiliating, intimidating or threatening
- **Abandonment** — desertion of a vulnerable elder by anyone who has assumed the responsibility for care or custody of that person
- **Self-neglect** — characterized as the failure of a person to perform essential, self-care tasks and that such failure threatens his/her own health or safety

WHO SPEAKS FOR TEXAS RESIDENTS?

Congress amended the Older Americans Act in 1978 to establish the Long-term Care Ombudsman program to serve residents in long-term care facilities. Ombudsman services are available in every state and territory of the United States. In Texas, the Office of the Long-term Care Ombudsman operates in the Texas Department of Aging and Disability Services.

"Elder abuse is an ongoing issue our ombudsmen work to prevent," said State Long-term Care Ombudsman. "Every resident deserves to live free of the fear, stress and physical toll of abuse. Retaliation is another common fear, which leads victims of abuse to remain silent.

"Every resident has a voice. Ombudsmen seek to empower and protect that right," she added.

Long-term care ombudsmen also advocate for resident quality of life and care including choosing the best residence in which to live. Federal and state authority mandates long-term care ombudsmen to:

- identify, investigate and resolve complaints made by, or on behalf of, residents and
- provide services to help in protecting resident health, safety, welfare and rights.

Many long-term care ombudsmen in Texas are

volunteers. To find out how to become a volunteer
ombudsman, call 1-800-252-2412 or visit the
DADS Long-term Care Ombudsman website.

WHAT TO DO IF YOU SUSPECT ABUSE

- If you suspect abuse, neglect or exploitation
  of an **older person living in a nursing
  home call 1-800-458-9858**.
- If you suspect abuse, neglect or exploitation
  of **any older person, call 1-800-252-5400**
  or report it online at
  https://www.txabusehotline.org.

ABOUT RESIDENTS' RIGHTS MONTH

Residents' Rights Month originated as Residents'
Rights Week in 1981 at a Consumer Voice annual
meeting. Several nursing home residents in
attendance from across the United States decided it
would be special for all residents if time were set
aside to celebrate residents and their rights,
separate from annual National Nursing Home
Week events always held in May. The Consumer
Voice organized a successful petition drive to
persuade Congress to designate a "Residents'
Rights Day."

Since 1981, the Consumer Voice has preserved the
tradition of celebrating Residents' Rights, and, in
2011, Residents' Rights Week was expanded to

Residents' Rights Month. This expansion provides additional time for residents, facility staff, family members, community advocates and ombudsmen to conduct educational programs and festive events to call attention to this important topic.

Report suspected waste, fraud or abuse in health and human services programs to the Texas State Auditor's Office
at 1-800-TX-AUDIT and to the HHSC Office of Inspector General at 1-800-436-6184.

03/28/2017

1. **UNIFORM**: WEAR TENNIS SHOES AND FRESHLY PRESSED UNIFORMS AT ALL TIMES! NO FILP FLOPS, NO SOCKS ONLY, NO BAREFEET.
2. **MEDICATION TIMES:** ARE SET! DO NOT CHANGE THE TIMES UNLESS APPROVED BY ME..............8:00 AM.......12:00 PM........2:00PM.............500 PM.............8:00 PM.......

Do not alter these times for any reasons. You must get a verbal approval from MRS.

WOODS only! ONLY ONE PERSON IS TO TOUCH THE MEDICATIONS FOR THE RESIDENTS PER SHIFT. If you are doing medication, do not take on any other task. TAKE ALL RESIDENTS THAT MAY NEED TO GO TO THE RESTROOM THERE FIRST SO THAT YOU ARE NOT DISTRACTED by a resident's family, another resident, a phone call, etc..... Allow the other person/staff to be on the floor and available to assist with the other residents. This is to AVOID any medication errors. Do not manage but one resident's medication at a time. Do not put medications in a resident's mouth. For feeders, you must figure a way to give them a treat with the medication inside, especially feeders. Do not put it in apple sauce or pudding if the resident cannot pick it up or hold it in their hands AND feed it to themselves. Example: get a cupcake cut it into enough pieces for a feeder, (you should have an order to crush) allow them to pick it up and put it in their mouth. It will take time and patience, but you are NOT TO ADMINISTER ANY MEDICATIONS. GET CREATIVE! FIGURE IT OUT. For non-feeders, put the medication in the lid of the bottle, on the plate where it will not fall off/out, and allow them to PICK IT UP. Either type resident, stay there and look inside the mouth to be sure they swallowed the medication.

3. ___*ERRORS CAN HAPPEN, NO MATTER HOW GOOD YOU BELIEVE YOU ARE, ALWAYS REPORT IT..................THIS COULD MEAN LIFE OR DEATH OF A RESIDENT!*___
   As for over the counter (NOT A PRESCRIPTION) creams, suppositories, ointments and eye drops we must discuss before using! Some we may do some we may not. ASK your manager.

4. **COMMUNICATION**: A) shift change B). If there is a change in resident care C). during your shifts
   You are a team of adults, act like it. We all have issues, no one is perfect. Try and work through the issues without forming opinions about each other. Do the right thing and no one can complain.

5. **PAY ATTENTION**: we are here to keep the residents safe and take care of 99 % of their needs. Each of you are needed, however you must follow the rules of ANCHOR WAY SENIOR CARE AND NOT DO YOUR OWN THING. Many of us walk around for hours and have not looked

to see if a resident's arm has been in an uncomfortable position, if they are breathing, if they have blue lips, if they are pale, if they are sweaty, if they are leaning to one side, if they are having seizures...........if they have left the building. This is unacceptable. **Know where your residents are at all times.**

6. **OUTSIDE**: DO NOT GO OUTSIDE at dark excessively! We are in the country and the varmints are much bigger here than in the city. Be careful when coming and going. I do not want any of you to be harmed either.

7. **WATER:** it is VERY IMPORTANT that we give residents plenty of water!!! I DO NOT KNOW HOW I CAN STRESS THIS ANYMORE! AT MEALS AND BETWEEN MEALS................... you have the cart, take the water to them in the chairs and keep them hydrated. THAT WOULD MEAN 6 GLASSES OF WATER PER DAY 8AM WITH BREAKFAST, 10 AM WITH SMALL SNACK, 12 NOON WITH LUNCH, 3PM WITH SNACK, 5PM WITH DINNER, AND LAST 8PM WITH SNACK AND MEDICAITONS. Please be sure the resident is DRINKING all the water....... ALL OF THE WATER. This

helps with hydration, skin, and avoid urinary tract infections. The whole cup each time filled to the top of the cup. No coffee and no juice before they swallow water. Do

8. **HOUSE CLEANING:** IN THE KITCHEN; SWEEP AND MOP AFTER EVERY MEAL. SWEEP AT END OF EVERY SHIFT IF YOU HAVE HAD SPILLS. MOP THE HALLWAYS THURSDAYS AND SATURDAYS. Keep the facility free of debris and smelling good. If it is broken, either get it repaired or replaced.

9. **LINENS**: CHANGE THE LINENS WHENEVER A RESIDENT has an accident in bed or while sitting in the designated areas. Linens must be changed EVERY FRIDAY with the night shift striping the beds as the morning staff get the residents up EVERY FRIDAY MORNING! Whether you are in the kitchen, bathroom, dining room......etc. If you make a spill, clean it up. Nail polish, trash, paper, mop strings, clean up behind yourself.

10. **BEDS:** DISINFECT THE BEDS every Friday with bleach and water. Wipe the rails, head and foot board and mattress.

11. **TOILETS:** DO NOT TAKE A RESIDENT TO THE TOILET without cleaning the toilet

after use. Every time someone uses the toilet, CLEAN AND DISINFECT IT!!! Especially when there was poop or blood.

12. **TRASH:** Empty trash after each shift and as needed. Straighten and organize the room. Lysol the trash can as needed.

13. **ACTIVITIES:** each shift, each day should do one activity with the residents for at least 30 minutes. .... EACH SHIFT!!! NO EXCEPTIONS...<u>YES INCLUDING THE NIGHT SHIFT</u>. You can do group or individual. When you use the supplies, place them back in the correct place. You all lose checkers, dominos, cards because you do not place them back in its rightful order/place/containers. ORGANIZE YOUR SHIFT!

14. **MEALS:** A resident must **have a** ½ - 1 cup of each vegetable, meat, bread of some type, water and if on the menu, a dessert. Do not take the plate off the table without making several attempts to get the resident to eat all their food. Do not feed heaping spoon full to the feeders/Teaspoon at a time is plenty. Be patient, organize your shift.

15. **SCHEDULES:** BE ON TIME! Follow the policy and procedure for switching out, taking off, and vacations. Know what they

are? You have 30 minutes to sit, eat, check your messages, chat on your phones…. with pay…. otherwise, find yourself busy doing something work related. Do not just hit and miss at a job duty, do it well. If there is not enough work for two staff members, why have them here? Then when I get to work, I see many things un-done?

16. **PERSONAL EMPLOYEE INFORMATION:** You must inform the manager anytime your personal information changes; especially addresses.

17. **DIABETICS**: this is a serious disease. Diabetes could cause serious kidney and heart issues (stroke/heart attacks). WHAT "YOU" feel?

18. **FAMILY PURCHASED FOODS**: DO NOT SHARE THE FAMILY PURCHASED. If a family member brings something special for their mom or dad, put their name on each pkg…IMMEDIATELY. Put it in the pantry to be issued by a designated on the day shift only. Discard all expired foods daily.

19. **DISHES AND COOKING**: If one staff is cooking the other will "later" do the dishes while the second person will watch the front which will only include group or individual

activities and restroom runs. Name the activities we have? Try and use dishes that are easy for an elder person to use.

DO NOT WASH DISHES UNTIL ALL RESIDENTS HAVE GONE TO THE RESTROOM AFTER BREAKFAST.... UNCH......DINNER............ (Empty crumbs into the trash) Stack the dishes & pots and pans neatly at the sink then take all residents to the restroom. The cooker will take half...the dish washer will take half......intermittently. AT all times keep a sharp eye on the residents; ORGANIZE YOUR SHIFT.

ALWAYS FOLLOW THE MENU. IF THERE ARE LEFTOVERS, THEY MUST BE SERVED ON THE 4TH DAY BY 5:00 P.M. or discarded. Put them in a bowl with the purchased cover, label it with the food name and date. Do not put foil on the container. Do not leave the container open. Do not leave drinks half empty with no lids. You must use it all or throw it away. Avoid throwing food away. Use it for the pureed meals.

Remember food temperatures: do not remove the thermometer from the refrigerator or freezer.

20. Note: Stay on top of activities. Activities are to promote socialization and movement vs sitting in the recliners most of the day. No one wants to walk in and see everyone asleep. There are many things' residents can do during the day. Most of all ask the residents what they would like to do. Many times, they may tell you, they are just fine.
21. Note: An assistant manager has been appointed; respect the title.
22. Note: do not leave wheelchairs in the bedrooms at night nor beside a chair. A RESIDENT MAY/WILL GET UP AND TRANSFER BY THEMSELVES AND FALL.

1. **MANAGE (SUPERVISE) MEDICATION FOR OUR RESIDENTS. This means place the medication in reach of the resident. They should pick it up and put it into their own mouth.**
2. YOU ARE *NOT TO PUT MEDICATION INTO ANY RESIDENT'S MOUTH NOR BODY* (ADMINISTER) unless you are a nurse or certified medication aide.
3. **FOR RESIDENTS YOU MUST FEED, SIMPLY FIND SOMETHING THEY LIKE TO EAT;** they are not able to feed themselves an entire meal, but they can grab a small piece of small snack. They must have an

order to crush medications. Crush the medication and put it on a small piece of cake, cookie, peanut butter and jelly sandwich or fruit and allow them to eat it.

4. THIS INCLUDES, SUPPOSITORIES, PILLS, LIQUID........................ ALL MEDICATIONS, follow these guidelines Please read the information provided and sign the bottom of each sheet. This is to acknowledge you have read, understand and will comply this information.

EMPLOYEE DIRECT DEPOSIT FORM

AUTHORIZATION FOR DIRECT DEPOSIT-EMPLOYEE FORM

This form authorizes **ANCHOR WAY SENIOR CARE, LLC** to send credit entries electronically or by any other commercially accepted method to my (our) account (s) indicated below and to other accounts I (we) identify in the future. This authorizes the financial institution holding the account to post all such entries.

PLEASE WRITE ABOVE THE LINES:

ACCOUNT TYPE:

(CIRCLE ONE) <u>CHECKING</u> OR <u>SAVINGS</u>

_____

BANK NAME (ABOVE)

BANK ROUNTING OR ABA # (ABOVE)

CHECKING OR SAVINGS ACCOUNT# (ABOVE)

PERCENTAGE OR DOLLAR AMOUNT TO BE DEPOSITED: 100%

This authorization will be in effect until ANCHOR WAY SENIOR CARE receives a new direct deposit form, written termination notices from myself and has a reasonable opportunity to act on it.

SIGNATURE_____

DATE _____

PRINTED _____

NAME_____

Final Thoughts

6

> *"The Eyes are the window to your soul"*
> **-- William Shakespeare**

I f you please the people you serve, others will come! *Inspect what you expect.* Know what is going on in your facility. Out of all these years, my advertisement has been minimal due to having word-of-mouth referrals.

As a final thought, a manager must be in the facility forty hours per week or be readily available. There were times when I noticed I was not receiving many messages correctly and often not at all. You don't want to miss calls from potential resident families. At a point, all telephone calls were routed to my cell phone.

Keep close contact with the families via phone calls and texts. This will set you apart from other owners. Feel free to send quick videos or video calls so that they may visit with their relatives during the day. Always get approval to show videos or photos on your website or social media in writing, but never include a resident's name. And keep your facility ODOR FREE!

Staff often have a habit of walking into a room and blurting out information, concerns, or personal situations on the floor. Educate them. Everything does not need to be said aloud, especially when there is another guest in the facility or the area, especially when you are a small facility. And never allow your staff to use words such as no, don't, stop, can't, not, etc. but train them to use kind words to redirect or offer other choices.

The ultimate goal is to make every family member feel welcome when they visit your facility. Whatever you promise a family or a resident, keep your word.

Be a great example for your staff. Dress to impress. Dress in the direction you are trying to go (*up*). Speak professionally to staff and others. Lead by example. Your staff has to buy in to your company. They have to help residents to the best of their ability; showing up for work is the best way to do that. MOREVER, allow your actions to be positive. Never ask your staff to do anything you would not do yourself. Let them see your business "*from your eyes.*"

ABOUT THE AUTHOR

Shelita Y. Woods was born in a small East Texas town with her parents and three beautiful sisters. Her dad was a great inspiration in many ways, especially concerning finances. He is now deceased, and cannot read the words within the pages of this book. Woods knows her dad is proud of her and sees the fruit of his labor through her business.

Wood's mother has shown her how to be a lady, wife, and mother. She is still here to share in this special phase of her life. Woods is the mother of two wonderful children: a daughter and a son. She has four grand-children who are the air that she breathes: two granddaughters and two grandsons. Woods is so proud of them that it makes her speechless.

It was a great choice for Shelita to move to the DFW area in 1984. She has truly been blessed to become a blessing to many. Woods shares her story partly because most biographies include higher education information from multiple universities. She has gotten where she is because of God's favor. Woods received her bachelor's degree while at Bank of America, she received her master's degree while at JP Morgan Chase, and she received her Ph.D. while at Anchor Way Senior Care.

Woods loves to travel to warm tropical cities. She is told that she is a leader who is strong and independent. Woods has a strong love for God, love, marriage, and family. She will give from her heart to someone in need, and she is thankful to her parents, grandparents, and great-grandparents for showing her love. Today, Woods can show that love for the elderly. God and ANCHOR WAY SENIOR CARE have blown Woods mind.

A Message from Shelita Y. Woods:

It was time to share what I have seen and experienced,

From My Eyes.

MY NOTES

ANCHORING MY DREAM

_____

_____

_____

_____

_____

_____

_____

_____

_____

www.ingramcontent.com/pod-product-compliance
Lightning Source LLC
Chambersburg PA
CBHW021626120626
46545CB00002B/422